Why I Will Never Buy an Electric Car

Colin M Barron

Published by Perthshire Publishing

Cover design by James Culver

Copyright © 2023 Colin M Barron

Author's website:

www.colinbarron.co.uk

Colin M Barron has asserted his right under the Copyright, Designs and Patents Act 198 to be identified as the author of this work.

ISBN 9798854383578

This work has been registered with the British Library and the American Library of Congress.

OTHER BOOKS BY COLIN M BARRON

NON-FICTION

Running Your Own Private Residential or Nursing Home

The Craft of Public Speaking

Planes on Film: 10 Favourite Aviation Films

Dying Harder: Action Movies of the 1980s

A Life By Misadventure

Battles on Screen: WW2 Action Movies

Practical Hypnotherapy

Victories at Sea: In Films and TV

Travels in Time: The Story of Time Travel Cinema

FICTION

Operation Archer

Codename Enigma

24 Hours to Doomsday

Four Minutes To Zero

CONTENTS

Introduction

By 2030, it will be impossible to buy a new petrol or diesel car in the UK. Five years later the sale of new hybrid cars will also be banned. Other countries in the developed world have adopted similar timetables for phasing out cars with internal combustion engines. This is being done to combat alleged 'man-made climate change' caused by C02 emissions from the burning of fossil fuels.

But, as I will explain in this book, there is considerable doubt as to whether man-made climate change really exists. Even if it does, it is likely that the effects of a modest increase in global temperatures will be beneficial to humankind. But you would not think this was the case from the alarmist headlines in the mainstream media. Furthermore, one of the perceived solutions to the problem — electric cars — will cause great problems. Because they are not cheap to buy or run, they are not really eco-friendly and they won't save the planet. In short, they are an impractical solution for a problem that doesn't exist as I shall explain in the following pages.

Chapter 1

The Greatest Day of My Life

What was the greatest day of my life? The day I met my wife, Vivien? Or the day we went on our first date? Or the day we got married in Cyprus, in 2002? Perhaps it might be the day I graduated in medicine in 1979? Or the day I passed my Primary FRCS examination in 1982? Or the day I got my first article published in a professional publication? Or the day in 1990, when my first book was published?

It was none of these days.

The greatest day of my life was 11 February 1974. The day I passed my driving test. I can still remember every detail of that event as though it was yesterday. The sky was overcast, but it was not raining and the temperature was mild for the time of year, probably about nine degrees Celsius. I remember holding the small white postcard, written with a blue biro, which gave details of the time and date of my test and the name of my examiner, who was Mr Best.

At 9.00 a.m., I left our house with my mother in her orange Renault 5TL, registration number XVS 571L, to drive to the test centre at the foot of Campbell Street, Greenock, close to the container terminal at Princes Pier. This gave us time to take a long route to our destination to ensure that the four-cylinder 956 cc engine was fully warmed up. In those days most petrol cars had carburettors incorporating a manually-operated *choke* which gave a richer mixture for starting the engine in the winter. Sometimes this could cause problems in the first few minutes of a journey as insufficient choke could make the engine stall. To avoid this potential problem we aimed to arrive at the test centre with a warm engine so that the choke knob didn't need to be pulled out.

The test started exactly on time and my examiner asked me to drive around Greenock while he checked that I was competent in all aspects of driving. Hill starts. Three-point turns. Reversing round corners. The correct use of mirrors and signals. Negotiating roundabouts. Emergency stops. And so on. After forty minutes we returned to the test centre where Mr Best quizzed me about the meaning of a number of traffic signs and asked me many questions about the Highway Code.

Then he ticked me off for making what he considered a superfluous signal during my test. I had indicated right because the road veered left and I wanted to go straight-ahead down a short road to arrive back at the test centre.

'I thought it was standard procedure,' I said.

'There is no such thing as standard procedure in driving, Mr Barron,' he replied.

I felt glum. He was going to fail me for a minor indiscretion. Then he spoke again.

'That's the end of your driving test, Mr Barron.' he said. 'And I'm very pleased to tell you that you've passed.'

Mr Best then gave me a small certificate to confirm that I had passed the test and told me to send it to the DVLA (Driver and Vehicle Licensing Agency), who would then issue me with a full licence.

Soon after this unexpected, but welcome achievement, we drove back to our family house in Golf Place. My mother departed in her Renault to go to work at Greenock Eye Infirmary, where she was employed as a consultant ophthalmologist and I walked downhill from Golf Place to Greenock Academy where I was a sixth-year pupil. To say I was on a high was something of an understatement. I couldn't wait to tell my classmates about my success.

One of the first people I told was my close friend, David, but instead of being overjoyed he was furious. A few weeks earlier he had predicted that he would pass his driving test the first time and I would not. He also told me that my allocated examiner, Mr Best, failed everyone. In reality the exact opposite to what he predicted had happened. He failed his driving test the first time he sat it and I did not.

'Mr Best passes everyone,' he said when he heard my news, momentarily forgetting that he had contradicted his previous prediction in a classic example of what I would now recognise as cognitive dissonance.

Despite David's annoyance at my success I remained elated. From that moment I grabbed every opportunity to drive. If one of our two family cars needed petrol I would volunteer to drive to the filling station. I offered to go shopping. I also volunteered to drive my GP father on his house calls around Greenock and Port Glasgow. This was how I gained most of my driving experience. I only ever had six lessons from a driving school. My instructor was called Mr Gunn, and he drove a silver Ford Escort Mark 1 with an 1100 cc engine. The rest of my driving experience came from taking my father on his house calls during evenings and weekends.

There was an even more exciting experience to savour. Until fairly recently my father had driven largely uninspiring cars. We had lived opposite Lang's Garage in Union Street, Greenock until September 1969. This was a Rootes, Hillman dealer and so over the years my father had bought a number of Hillman Minx cars and also three of the ghastly, poorly built, rear-engine Hillman Imps, which were constructed at the nearby strike-prone Linwood factory. My father also bought a few dreary cars made by BMC, later British Leyland, such as the Mini, the Maxi and the Austin 1100. These were technically interesting designs but marred by poor build quality.

Then in September 1972, my father visited the only Volvo dealer in Greenock, Westfield Garage at the top of Campbell Street, owned by a man called Reg Knight. My father had intended to buy a Volvo 144, a sturdy and comfortable two-litre saloon, which was popular in Greenock at the time. Instead, he spotted a beautiful new car sitting in the showroom and fell in love with it instantly.

My father had never been that interested in cars before as was shown by his purchase of rather unexciting vehicles manufactured by Hillman, BMC and British Leyland. But the Volvo 164 was different.

Based on the 144, the 164 had an extended front end to incorporate a powerful six-cylinder, three litre, straight-six engine, which delivered 145 bhp. This would be considered a puny power output for a modern three-litre engine, but by 1972 standards it was impressive. The car was beautifully trimmed with soft black leather seats, which had a wonderful aroma and thick high-quality carpets. These were probably the most comfortable car seats I have ever sat in. Since the mid-sixties Volvo had used an orthopaedic surgeon to help them design their seats. Another luxury feature was a sliding metal sunroof worked by a window winder-type handle. The car was painted in a light-blue, metallic finish with additional chrome trim in comparison to a 144, which had stainless steel wheel trims and tinted windows. The front end was particularly impressive with a square radiator grille flanked by two spotlamps that made it look like a Daimler.

In March 1974, my parents, very generously, had me added as a named driver for the Volvo. So now I could drive around Greenock in one of two cars, an orange Renault 5TL, or a huge, light-blue metallic Volvo with tinted windows. My self-esteem and my standing among my classmates soared. To say I was on a high was an understatement. One of my most treasured memories from that period was in April 1974, when I drove from Greenock to Inverkip along the coast road. The sun was shining. The sky was blue. There was little traffic. The sunroof was open and the car radio was playing the current number one, *Seasons in the Sun* by Terry Jacks. It was one of the happiest moments of my life.

On 20 July 1974, I travelled to the Strathallan aircraft collection near Auchterarder in Perthshire in the Renault 5TL, to attend an air display of historic aircraft, which included a Spitfire and a Hurricane. Accompanying me were two of my school friends, Ewan McLean and Maggie Henderson, who are now both deceased.

I will always treasure the memory of that day. I don't have any photos of that event, but a film of that display can be seen on You Tube. The only way to get to that small grass airfield in the middle of nowhere was by motor car as public transport in that area was poor. So passing my driving test changed my life and gave me freedom. A freedom that governments around the world are now planning to take away from us, as you will discover from reading this book.

In retrospect it was no surprise that I passed my driving test first time. Because I have always been a *petrolhead*. I have always enjoyed driving cars, washing and polishing cars, reading about cars, visiting car shows and watching TV documentaries about cars. I used to visit the bi-annual Scottish Motor Show when it was held in Glasgow's Kelvin Hall, and in later years at the Scottish Exhibition Centre. I still attend the annual classic car show in Bridge of Allan, a few miles from my house.

When I was at Glasgow University studying medicine I became the editor of *SURGO* (*Glasgow University Medical Journal*) in 1977. One of the first changes I made was to introduce a motoring section featuring road tests. Originally this was written by my brother Alastair under the pen-name *Fanny Belt*, but after a year when Alastair was no longer available I became *Fanny Belt* and wrote several road tests using this *nom de plume*. The motoring pages in *SURGO* proved a success and lead to motor dealers placing adverts which helped to pay for the magazine. SURGO was given free to all, 1000-plus medical students at Glasgow University and was funded entirely by advertising revenue.

A few years later — I was by then a junior doctor — I became involved with another publication called *Glasgow Medicine* and had a number of roles. Officially, I was the art editor and was responsible for cover design, cartoons, graphics and page layout. But I also wrote a few articles for the publication and became its motoring correspondent, and road tested many cars. By this time I had acquired a 35 mm Canon T70 SLR camera so I also took the photos which accompanied the road test.

Incidentally, the very first thing I ever had published in a professional magazine was a poem entitled *Ode to a Mini,* which was printed in the June 1974 edition of *Car* magazine when I was seventeen. This is how it read:

There is upon our British Roads

A car that's very tinny

It's fifteen years out of date

The British Leyland Mini

Its paintwork is very poor

Its driving position is bad

And the seats! They must have been designed

By the Marquis De Sade

Safety features has it none

The engine makes a din

And the only time it makes you glad

Is when you trade it in

But if your wallet's very light

And have a car you must

Then go ahead and buy a Mini

And watch it turn to rust

Most cars possess a glovebox

Of size one cubic foot

The Mini's got one too, of course

Only it's called the boot!

The instruments are badly placed

It's hard to shut the door

You're better just to trade it in

And buy a Renault Four.

***

I have also had the pleasure of driving a number of interesting vehicles over nearly fifty years of car ownership. These include the following — two Renault 5TLs, a Renault 5 GT Turbo, three Toyota MR2s, two Volvo 760 Turbos, a Jaguar XJ6 Sovereign, a Daimler Six, a Citroen Xantia V6 auto, a Jaguar X-type saloon and a Jaguar X-type Sovereign Estate. I loved them all.

I have mentioned all these facts about my life purely to emphasize that — with my great interest in motor cars and engines — I feel I am qualified to comment on the government's plans to phase out petrol and diesel cars. I say this because, during the Covid pandemic I was among a small minority in the population who was critical of the government's response. On a number of occasions I found myself arguing on social media with people who had no medical or scientific degrees and no respect for my qualifications. Here are some of the comments I received:

"One look at your Facebook page tells me everything I need to know. You're a hypnosis nutter!" This referred to the fact that I worked as a clinical hypnotherapist for sixteen years and even wrote a book on the subject.

"You're retired and you've never worked on a Covid ward so you don't know what you're talking about."

"You're an idiot! There is no evidence that facemasks cause infections!" My response — no I'm not an idiot and there *is* evidence that facemasks can cause infections and don't work.

I should add that I am also very interested in science and always have been. My best subjects at school were physics and chemistry and I won a number of science prizes, so I believe I have as much right as anyone else to question government policies on electric cars and also man-made global warming, the evidence for which is poor and in subsequent chapters I will discuss these issues in greater detail.

Chapter 2

A Brief History of "Horseless Carriages" and Engines

Humans originally walked everywhere, but by Biblical times animals such as horses and mules were used as transport. Carts pulled by oxen, and other cattle, were also employed. By the Middle Ages horse-drawn coaches and buggies were popular.

By the end of the 18th century the steam engine had been invented. This was subsequently improved by James Watt and other engineers. Early steam engines were used solely to pump water in mines, but by the early 19th century the first steam locomotives running on iron rails appeared. Progress in this field was rapid and by the 1840s, a huge railway infrastructure had been created in Britain, and subsequently in other countries throughout the world.

Steam-powered wagons, which could be driven along roads, were also designed. The first self-propelled steam machine still in existence is the Cugnot steam tractor which was built by French military engineer, Nicolas-Joseph Cugnot in 1769. It was designed to tow artillery pieces to the battlefield. A 2.5 tonne three-wheeled vehicle, it had a top speed of 2.5 mph and carried three passengers. It can still be seen at the Musée des Arts et Métiers in Paris. According to the Guinness World Records the first true steam car was the La Marquise, a four-wheeled, four-seater vehicle made by De Dion Bouton et Trépardoux of France in 1884.

Another pioneer in the world of steam vehicles was my ancestor William Murdoch. Born in Cumnock in Ayrshire, he later moved to England, where he worked for Boulton and Watt. In 1784, Murdoch demonstrated a working steam-powered horseless carriage in miniature form. Another of Murdoch's inventions was the pneumatic tube message system, which is still used today.

Early steam road vehicles had metal or wooden wheels and either no tyres or ones made of solid rubber and so offered a hard ride. But the invention of the Dunlop pneumatic tyre and smooth tarmacadam roads in the 19th century made wheeled steam vehicles more practical and comfortable.

Nonetheless, steam vehicles had a number of snags. Their engines were heavy and bulky and had a poor power-to-weight ratio compared with later internal combustion engines. They required a large water-filled boiler which had to be heated for some time to generate sufficient steam pressure to power the engine. Thus, the driver of a steam car or lorry would have to wait up to an hour for the boiler to heat up fully before starting the engine. Also, if the vehicle was involved in a crash, which burst the boiler, then the driver and passengers would be scalded by boiling water, sometimes with fatal consequences. The performance of steam vehicles was poor, with weak acceleration and a low top speed. The usual fuel was coal, although they could also be fired with wood, peat or oil. Despite these many drawbacks steam-powered cars continued to be manufactured in the UK until the 1930s, with the best-known model being the Stanley Steamer.

Petrol (gasoline) Cars

A more promising development was the invention of the internal combustion engine. Several pioneers are credited with the creation of such power plants from the late 18th century onwards and some were fitted in road vehicles. However, the father of the motor car is generally accepted as being the German, Karl Benz, who patented a two-stroke, petrol engine in 1879, and built what we now recognize as the first motor cars in 1886. These early vehicles had relatively powerless engines, but as the 20th century unfolded, power output, top speed and acceleration steadily increased.

The invention of the internal combustion engine also lead to the Wright Brothers' first powered flight in 1903. Winged flying machines had been proposed in the 19th century, but all attempts to make an aircraft powered by a steam engine fly, proved fruitless as such engines were too heavy and bulky for aviation use, with a poor power-to-weight ratio. Various inventors attempted to make a steam-powered aircraft fly, including Hiram Maxim in 1894, who was best known for the Maxim gun, which was adopted by many nations, including Britain. The First World War, 1914–18, lead to a quantum leap in engine technology with average engine power greatly increasing, particularly in aircraft.

One way to increase engine power was to have more cylinders. Some early petrol engines had a single cylinder, but engines with two, three, four, five, six, eight and even twelve cylinders have been developed for use in cars, while some aircraft engines have even more cylinders. The Napier-Sabre engine, used in the RAF's WW2 Hawker Typhoon and Tempest fighters had twenty-four cylinders. Another invention was the air-cooled radial engine in which the cylinders were mounted in a radial pattern around the main crankshaft. One or two rows of cylinders could be fitted. This type of engine was mainly used in aircraft although some land vehicles employed them such as the revolutionary Tucker Torpedo car and some versions of the M4 Sherman tank and the earlier M3 Grant/Lee tank.

Another way of increasing engine power is to fit a supercharger or turbocharger. These are both ways of *blowing* air into an engine under pressure, thus increasing power. This is particularly useful in aircraft as it enables engine power to be maintained at high altitude where the air is thin.

A supercharger is driven mechanically by the crankshaft while a turbocharger is powered by the gas pressure of the engine exhaust. These devices were developed between the two world wars for aircraft use but were subsequently used in cars such as the famous 1931, *Blower* Bentley, which used an Amherst-Villiers supercharger. Turbochargers were first used in saloon cars in the late 1970s, with Saab being one of the first manufacturers to employ them. A problem with early turbocharged cars was 'Turbo lag' in which there was a delay between pressing the accelerator and the turbo reaching full revs, but modern electronic engine management systems have lessened this problem.

Another way of increasing engine power is to inject methanol or nitrous oxide, 'laughing gas', into the cylinders to give a brief burst of extra power. This was used in WW2 in some fighter aircraft, but although it has been used in a number of racing cars it has never been used in production motor vehicles.

The Diesel Engine

This is the other main type of internal combustion engine and was invented by Rudolf Diesel, in 1892, and patented in 1895. The main difference between the diesel engine and the earlier petrol (gasoline) engine is that diesels use a thicker hydrocarbon fuel, called diesel oil. In the original design of the petrol engine, fuel is mixed with air in a device called a carburettor. The resulting vapour then enters the engine cylinder where it is compressed by a piston and then ignited electrically by a spark plug. The resulting combustion of the fuel/air mixture and the consequent massive expansion of gases drives the piston down and turns the crankshaft. In modern vehicles the carburettor is replaced by electronically controlled fuel injection. In the diesel engine; however, the fuel/air mixture is compressed sufficiently to generate heat and it is this which ignites the fuel rather than a spark plug. Modern diesel engines are fitted with a device called a glow plug, but this has a different function to a spark plug. A spark plug ignites the fuel/air mixture, but the glow plug merely heats the cylinder to aid initial starting, particularly in cold weather.

The main advantage of the diesel engine is greatly increased fuel economy and reduced running costs, compared with a petrol engine. The main disadvantages are the smell from the fuel, the odour from the exhaust and the engine noise, which is not as pleasant as that emitted by a multi-cylinder petrol engine. Acceleration is also poorer compared with a petrol car of the same cubic capacity although modern diesels have had various technical tweaks to improve their performance, with the fitting of turbochargers being common. Modern upmarket diesel cars also have more pleasant and unobtrusive engine sounds compared with early diesels. So the performance gap between diesel and petrol cars of the same cubic capacity is not as great as it was in the sixties.

Diesel cars and commercial vehicles have been around for over a hundred years. But it is relatively recently that they have achieved market dominance, before sales declined because of bad publicity about exhaust emissions. During WW2 most cars, vans, trucks and tanks ran on petrol rather than diesel. There's a line in the 1970 movie *Patton* in which General Omar Bradley, played by Karl Maldern, discusses the US Army's defeat at the Battle of Kasserine Pass in 1943. One explanation he offers is that German tanks had diesel engines, i.e. less inflammable, whereas American tanks were all gasoline, (petrol)-fuelled and likely to catch fire when hit.

Actually, this is untrue, during WW2, *all* German tanks and armoured vehicles were powered by petrol engines while the Allies used both petrol and diesel-power plants. The most numerous US tank, the M4 Sherman, was made in both petrol and diesel versions. The British Valentine tank was also made in petrol and diesel variants while the Crusader, Cromwell and Comet tanks were only made with petrol engines. The ubiquitous Willys Jeep was only manufactured with a Go Devil petrol engine, although its modern counterparts are diesel.

Incidentally, the Cromwell and Comet tanks, plus the Centurion, which just missed seeing action in WW2, were all powered by the same engine, the Rolls-Royce Meteor. This was essentially a Rolls-Royce Merlin aircraft engine, as used in the Spitfire, with the supercharger removed. This had a power output of 600 horsepower, compared with 1000 to 1600 horsepower for the aircraft version, which was adequate for tanks of that era.

Even as late as the 1970s, many trucks were still petrol-fuelled. The Bedford RL, based on the civilian Bedford model S, which was the British Army's standard three-ton truck from the early 50s until the late 70s, had a six-cylinder petrol engine and was never manufactured with a diesel. Similarly the 1970s Ford Transit van was available with a V4 petrol engine, the same unit that was fitted to some models of the Ford Consul. So the market dominance of the diesel vehicle really only started in the 1980s. Almost all current vans and lorries are diesel-powered with some electric vans starting to appear.

Jet Engines, Gas Turbines and Turbo-props

A 'jet engine' and a 'gas turbine' are essentially the same thing. Their invention is credited to Frank Whittle, an RAF officer who patented his creation in 1932. As with most inventions, a number of people were working on similar ideas around the same time. Thus the Germans produced the world's first jet aircraft, the Heinkel He178, which first flew on 27 August 1939. Whittle's first jet prototype, the Gloster E28/39 flew almost two years later on 15 May 1941.

Even in the 1920s, Whittle realised that propeller-driven aircraft with petrol engines had their limitations. The problem was that the internal combustion engine produced less power as it ascended to a greater altitude where the air was thinner. The propeller also became less effective at great height.

Whittle proposed a much simpler engine design known as the gas turbine in which fuel and air were drawn into a series of *burner cans* arranged inside a cylindrical engine. The fuel/air mixture was compressed and then ignited resulting in a massive expansion of gases which caused a jet blast out the rear of the engine. These hot gases drove a turbine at the rear which was linked by a shaft to a fan at the front of the engine which sucked in more air. Once the engine was started by spinning the shaft it would keep running until the fuel supply was cut off.

The jet engine offered the possibility of tremendous thrust and actually worked better in the thin air found at high altitude. It also had few moving parts compared with an internal combustion engine and thus produced little vibration. One problem with 1940s aircraft piston engines was that they were immensely complicated with a large number of cylinders and thousands of moving parts which could all be moving in different directions, and causing tremendous noise and vibration.

A further development was the so-called turboprop, also known as the jet-prop; when fitted in helicopters it is known as a turboshaft. I mentioned earlier that a jet engine has two fans, one at the front and one at the rear, joined by a driveshaft. If you can imagine the drive shaft extended forward ahead of the engine nacelle and fitted with a propellor then you have a turboprop. A further refinement is the fitting of a reduction gearbox to slow down the propeller because jet engines turn over so fast that an ungeared propeller would exceed the speed of sound. Turboprops produce most of their thrust through the propeller but still have some residual jet thrust from the exhaust at the rear of the engine nacelle.

Early turboprops were developed during WW2, but the first really successful design was the Rolls-Royce Dart which was fitted to the world's first turboprop airliner the Vickers Viscount, which first flew in 1948. The aircraft was originally called the Viceroy, but the name was changed to Viscount because of India's new independent status.

The Viscount proved a huge success, with 445 built and many exported. It was fast, with a cruising speed of about 350 mph, which was 100 mph faster than the speediest piston-engine airliners. It was also quieter, with a vibration-free cabin, large comfortable seats and huge oval windows, a feature that is not found in modern airliners.

At that time the Americans didn't have a turboprop-powered airliner in development. The main American turboprop airliner was the Lockheed L-188 Electra, which did not fly until 1957, so the British were leading the world. The main advantage of a turboprop over a pure jet is that it is much more fuel efficient, and hence more economical for short and medium-length journeys than a pure jet.

In 1952, the British aircraft industry produced a much larger turboprop airliner known as the Bristol Britannia. This had the potential to be a world-beater, but unfortunately, problems with the new and initially unreliable Bristol Proteus engines delayed its entry into service until 1957. The Britannia was the first airliner that could fly from London to New York without refuelling. Prior to that, trans-Atlantic flights had to be made using either a northern route, via Iceland, Greenland, Nova Scotia et cetera, or via a southern route stopping at the Azores and the Caribbean et cetera to permit refuelling.

By the time the Britannia's engine problems were sorted out, the new, and far superior, all-jet Boeing 707 had entered production. BOAC bought a fleet of Britannias, but within a few years, they were replaced with faster and larger Boeing 707s. In the early 1950s, Britain also looked set to lead the world with the first jet airliner, the de Havilland Comet, but a series of fatal crashes caused by metal fatigue forced a re-design of the aircraft and damaged its reputation. As a result the Boeing 707 became the world's leading long-range jet airliner from the early sixties onwards.

A similar fate awaited the Viscount's *big brother* the huge Vickers Vanguard, which first flew in 1959, and entered service in 1961. This was effectively an elongated version of the Viscount with four powerful Rolls-Royce Tyne turboprop engines. It was not a great success. Just 44 were built as only BEA (British European Airways) and TCA (Trans Canada Airlines) bought it. It had the same huge picture windows as the Viscount, and offered a 400-mph cruising speed, but this was slower than pure jets, and by the 1970s most of the surviving Vanguards had been converted to freighters, with the last being retired in 1996.

Ramjets and Pulse Jets

These are simpler forms of jet engine. The ramjet lacks a fan and turbine and can only be ignited when it is in forward motion. Ramjets have been used to provide additional propulsion to aircraft and some missiles such as the Bristol Bloodhound.

The pulse jet is a simple form of jet engine which was used in the German V-1 flying bomb. It is similar to the ramjet but has a set of opening shutters at the front of the cylindrical engine. These open to admit air and then close prior to ignition of the fuel/air mixture, which then drives the missile forward. The V-1 was usually started by being catapulted off a long ramp to provide the initial forward motion required for the engine to start. The frequent opening and closing of the shutters meant the thrust was delivered in a series of *pulses* giving the V-1 its characteristic *buzzing* sound.

Gas Turbines in Land Vehicles

Gas turbine engines with mechanical drive shafts and pure jet engines have both been used in land vehicles. A number of experimental racing cars have been fitted with gas turbines such as Donald Campbell's high-speed Proteus-powered car, the Bluebird CN7, which was built for an attempt on the land speed record and was capable of 400 mph. Campbell also owned a racing boat, the Bluebird K7, which was powered by a Metropolitan-Vickers Beryl turbojet engine.

Campbell lost his life in this boat on Coniston Water on 2 January 1967. In 2001, the Bluebird was salvaged from Coniston Water and restored to running condition in 2008.

In 1952, the Rover car company produced an experimental gas-turbine car, the Rover JET 1, to test the feasibility of this type of engine in a land vehicle. Other manufacturers have also built experimental gas-turbine cars. So far, gas turbines have not proved practical for ordinary motor cars because of their high fuel consumption, but they have been used in tanks, which require a very powerful engine because of their weight.

The American M1 Abrams tank, and subsequent variants, is powered by a 1500 horsepower gas-turbine engine. This gives it tremendous speed, fifty miles per hour or more on a good road. However, one snag of the Abrams is that it is a gas guzzler. This was particularly problematic in early versions, which lacked an auxiliary power unit (APU), a small engine attached to an electric generator that provides electric power when the tank's main engine is stopped. Abrams' tanks have since been retro-fitted with an APU, but high fuel consumption remains a problem with the M1 series being one of the few tanks in the world not powered by a diesel engine.

Electric Cars

Finally we come to the subject of electric cars. They first appeared as long ago as the 19th century with Robert Anderson being credited with the creation of one sometime between 1832 and 1839. By the end of the 20th century there were fleets of electric taxis in both London and New York.

So at the beginning of the 20th century there were four methods for propelling *horseless carriages,* namely petrol and diesel internal combustion engines, steam engines and electric cars powered by rechargeable batteries, which at that time were lead/acid accumulators.

Steam engines fell out of favour by the 1930s, for the reasons described earlier. The introduction of the electric starter made petrol and diesel engines the preferred choice for most motorists. But some electric cars persisted during the 20th century.

For example, the humble electric milk float powered by rechargeable lead/acid batteries was widely used until the 1970s. In those days most milk was delivered in reusable glass bottles to householders' doorsteps as depicted in Benny Hill's classic 1971 pop hit *Ernie, the Fastest Milkman in the West,* the video of which you can see on You Tube. This was an ideal application for an electric vehicle as a slow-moving truck with a short range was adequate for the task and charging could be done at a depot overnight. At the time of writing it looks as though milk in reusable glass bottles with home deliveries via electric carts may become a familiar sight on British streets again.

Electric vehicles in general have also made a comeback in the last decade because of the advent of rechargeable lithium batteries and the *climate change* scare and in the chapters which follow I will discuss this development in greater detail.

Chapter 3

The War on Cars

We have all heard of the War on Cancer, the War on Terror, the War on Obesity, the War on Poverty, The War on Drugs and so on. But governments around the world have been silently waging another war for several decades, namely the War on Cars.

The British Government is one of the worst offenders. Most people would consider the invention of the motor car to be one of the defining moments of the 19th century. Cars powered by internal combustion engines brought freedom to billions of people around the world and greatly enhanced their quality of life. But a number of politicians and activists see things differently. They view cars as a curse on humanity. Expensive, dangerous machines, which use up valuable natural resources, pollute the atmosphere and spew out vast quantities of carbon dioxide, a substance they regards as a *poison* as it allegedly causes global warming, which will eventually lead to a 'climate apocalypse' if unchecked. The fact that all animals, including humans, breathe out carbon dioxide seems to have escaped their notice. But as we all witnessed during the Covid pandemic, most politicians are scientifically illiterate.

All governments in the developed world are involved in the war on cars to some extent. The Scottish Government, for example, was forced into an alliance with the Green Party in order to have a working majority. Part of the deal was that two unelected Green ministers were to be appointed, namely Lorna Slater and Patrick Harvie. Slater's remit is Transport, while Harvie is involved in the 'decarbonisation' of buildings, which really means he will be persuading property owners to fit expensive heat pumps to replace their existing efficient gas boilers.

The Greens have also persuaded the Scottish Government to halt its road building programme with only upgrades urgently required for safety reasons being allowed to proceed. At the moment a contentious issue is the A9 road which runs between Perth and Inverness. Despite being one of the most important routes in Scotland with heavy traffic, much of it is still single carriageway. The total length of the A9 is eighty-eight miles, but only eleven miles are dual carriageway. As a result the A9 is one of Scotland's most dangerous roads with thirteen people killed on the route in 2022. In February

2023, Scottish Transport Secretary, Jenny Gilruth, admitted that the work to upgrade the A9 was behind schedule. The previously agreed target of 2025, to modernise the road would not be met. The A75 in southern Scotland also needs to be upgraded as it serves Stranraer, which is one of Scotland's most important ports.

The Scottish Government has made no secret of its desire to see cars phased out from Scotland's roads. Speaking in the Scottish Parliament in February 2023, Energy and Net Zero Minister, Michael Matheson, said that "the era of unconstrained car use is over".

The Welsh Government has also adopted similar policies. Recently it announced that road construction in Wales, apart from essential safety upgrades, would be halted because of the 'climate crisis.'

The UK Government has adopted similar policies. For the last few decades it has gradually introduced new rules and taxes to make life harder for motorists. Fuel Duty is at an all-time high, as is Road Tax. The introduction of low-emission zones means that many city centres are now *no-go* areas for most motorists. Only taxi drivers with relatively new vehicles, which meet the latest emission standards, can now go into many city centres. Electric taxis are available for purchase but are too expensive for most cabbies to consider.

The next stage in the war on cars will be the introduction of permanent 'climate lockdowns' in which residents will be required to stay within a short distance of their house and not travel. This is already being rolled out in some English cities such as Oxford and Bath. Many other towns and cities throughout the UK will adopt these policies. The Scottish Government has also indicated that it will implement similar plans, which will initially be introduced in Scotland's four largest cities namely Glasgow, Edinburgh, Perth and Aberdeen.

I believe the plan is to replace all internal combustion engine cars with electric cars before phasing them out as well. Politicians of all parties throughout the Western World do not like the idea of private car ownership since it conflicts with their plan for a New World Order in which the ownership of any private property will be banned. "You will own nothing and be happy", policies which are currently endorsed by the World Economic Forum and the United Nations.

In future, people will be encouraged to travel everywhere on foot or by bicycle. Limited public transport will be available. On the few occasions that a car is required, such as to take a disabled or elderly person to hospital or to a dental surgery, then a suitable electric self-driving car will be rented for that journey only using a smartphone app.

Now I must admit that I enjoy walking and cycling. From 1970 to 1976, one of my favourite leisure pursuits was hill walking. Since 1976, I have been a keen cyclist and have even been on cycling holidays, and stayed at youth hostels and bed and breakfasts and carried everything I needed in two pannier bags fitted either side of my bike's rear wheel.

In July 1977, I went on a long cycling holiday. I started in Greenock, where I used to live, and ended up in Inverness. I had originally planned to reach John o' Groats and then get the train back to Greenock. Unfortunately, the weather deteriorated after a week. I was soaked to the skin and had to return home to Greenock by train from Inverness.

This is one snag of cycling. It is really only a fair-weather activity. There is nothing more enjoyable than cycling in the country on quiet roads on a warm summer's day. But cycling when it is cold, icy, snowy, wet, foggy, dark or windy is unpleasant. Suggesting that everyone should walk or cycle everywhere regardless of the weather or the time of day is a cruel and ridiculous suggestion. But that is what is being proposed with the barmy 15-minute cities' plan.

So under these proposals 85-year-olds with heart problems will be required to walk 15 minutes to the shops every day to get food and then return to their rented *rabbit-hutch* home clutching their provisions. What the government plans for everyone is a cruel, miserable world where all joy has been eliminated in the name of 'climate justice'. And it doesn't matter what political party you vote for, they *all* support these plans. So be warned.

Chapter 4

Why Electric Cars are *Not* Green

Politicians and climate change activists have advocated the widespread adoption of electric cars because they are *eco-friendly* and will "save the planet". In reality, they are not at all eco-friendly, and will have no effect on man-made climate change — that is if it even exists. It is true that electric cars do not emit toxic emissions from their exhaust pipes like cars fitted with internal combustion engines. But in assessing whether electric cars are truly eco-friendly, we have to take into account the amount of carbon emissions produced during their construction.

The bodywork of an electric car is made of steel, which requires coal and iron, and a vast quantity of water and electricity, for its manufacture. The interior is made of more steel, plus plastic, which is made from oil. The electric motors are made of iron, steel, plastic, rubber and copper, which are already in short supply. Rare metals such as silver and gold are also used in the manufacture of the motors.

But it is the huge lithium battery, the size of a king-size mattress and weighing 500 kg, which makes electric cars very *eco-unfriendly*. These monstrosities require large quantities of rare metals, including lithium and cobalt. It is believed that there are insufficient quantities of these rare metals in the entire world to meet the likely future demand for batteries.

Let me give you some figures on what is required to make one 500 kg lithium battery. Ten tonnes of lithium salt have to be processed to produce the pure metal. Fifteen tonnes of ore are required to generate the cobalt. Two tonnes of ore for nickel and twelve tonnes of copper ore. In total two hundred tonnes of various ores and salts have to be processed to make one battery, resulting in more pollution than a petrol or diesel car generates in twenty years.

Currently in the UK there are 33 million private cars on the road. So if the government goes ahead with its 'Net Zero' plans, *all* future vehicles will need a huge lithium battery which currently costs between £8,000 and £10,000 and has to be replaced every 8 –10 years and can become less efficient after just a few years. And don't forget the plan is to have buses, coaches, taxis, lorries, vans, ambulances, fire engines, police vehicles, construction vehicles and bin lorries powered by these hugely expensive lithium batteries. Battery-powered buses and taxis are already operating in some parts of Britain, particularly London, the centre of which is now a *low emission zone.* Hybrid trains have also been mooted with a diesel engine charging a huge lithium battery.

Lithium batteries cannot be recycled or reconditioned, so once batteries for the *first wave* of electric vehicles have expired after five to ten years, further lithium and cobalt will have to be found and mined. Much of this mining takes place in the Congo, which uses child labourers working in deplorable conditions.

 Shortage of lithium and cobalt could be a problem as the world is running out of a lot of natural resources. Things have become so bad that China is now considering space missions to the Moon to recover rare and valuable minerals which are desperately needed on Earth. Apparently the Chinese believe they can bring back forty-five tons of cargo on each mission using a new type of spacecraft.

The shipping industry will also have its problems. At the start of the 19th century ships were powered by wind-driven sails. Then coal-fired steam piston engines supplanted and eventually replaced wind power. By the early 20th century the more efficient and powerful Parsons steam turbines replaced steam engines. Then coal-fired engines began to be replaced by oil-burning steam turbines. Nowadays, most ships are powered by vast diesel engines which consume huge quantities of fuel. It has even been suggested that in the future ships could be powered by rechargeable lithium batteries, which would greatly increase the demand for this rare and precious metal and also require vast amounts of electricity for charging.

At present mining for lithium and cobalt generates a huge amount of carbon emissions as the machinery involved is powered by fossil fuels, either directly or indirectly through electricity generation via fossil fuels. The lithium is then loaded onto diesel trucks and taken to ports where it is transported to the developed world in enormous diesel-powered ships.

This convoluted process means that the production of lithium batteries creates huge carbon emissions and this has to be taken into account when assessing whether electric vehicles are eco-friendly or not. Thus, electric car production causes far greater CO_2 emissions than the manufacture of equivalent petrol or diesel models. Indeed it has been calculated that the average petrol or diesel car would have to drive 50,000 miles before it produced as much C02 as a newly manufactured electric car.

Furthermore, electric cars would only be eco-friendly if the charging electricity they used was generated by something other than fossil fuels. Green campaigners seem to believe that electric cars are solely charged by electricity generated by 'renewables' such as solar power, wind farms, tidal power stations, hydro power and so on. In fact, most electricity generation in the UK is still via fossil fuels with 'renewables' only contributing a small percentage. Writing in the *Daily Mail* on 21 January 2023, Andrew Neil pointed out that 50% of the UK's electricity was currently generated by gas-fired power stations and only 17% by wind. All British coal-fired power stations were supposedly closed down years ago, with some even being demolished, but five of them have been reactivated in England to help with the current energy crisis. The Scottish Government has no plans to reopen closed coal, oil or nuclear power plants as it intends that all future electricity generation will use renewables. It has also declared that no new nuclear power plants will be built.

Wind power is particularly unreliable as wind turbines do not generate electricity when the wind does not blow. In order to prevent electricity blackouts, fossil fuel power stations have to be kept on standby to kick in when required. Wind turbines also have to be turned off to prevent damage when the wind speed is too high. The construction of these huge, ugly, bird-killing monstrosities is also distinctly eco-unfriendly as they require huge quantities of steel which can only be produced using coal.

Another way in which electric cars are not eco-friendly is that they contribute to atmospheric pollution via increased tyre wear. As I mentioned earlier, electric vehicles weigh an average of 500 kg more than petrol or diesel cars because of the weight of the battery. This causes increased tyre wear which means that tyres have to be replaced more often. Production of tyres involves carbon emissions and oil. In addition, increased tyre wear causes atmospheric pollution as tiny rubber particles get into the air. The increased tyre wear with electric cars means that tyres will have to be changed more often, pushing up running costs, and the government is reportedly looking at a *tyre tax*.

The government's plan is to force people to buy electric cars and ban petrol and diesel ones. I believe that electric cars will eventually be banned as well, perhaps because of concern about atmospheric pollution caused by tyre wear as it is clearly the intention of most governments to totally ban private car ownership.

Millions of perfectly serviceable petrol and diesel cars will be taken off our roads by government policies and will be sold to Third World Countries who don't seem concerned about climate change as they have more pressing problems to deal with such as feeding their population and growing their economy.

Another consequence of the increased weight of electric cars is that they cause more damage to other cars, and injury to pedestrians, in the event of an accident. There have also been concerns about the increased weight of electric cars causing multi-storey and underground car parks to collapse as such structures are not designed to take the weight of such heavy vehicles. Writing in the *Mail on Sunday* on 18 December 2023, Isolde Walters cited a report by the British Parking Association which stated that electric vehicles typically weighed an average of two tons, not just because of the weight of the battery but also because of heavy structural members added to the car bodyshell to support it. For example, the Tesla Model 3 weighs 2.2 tons fully loaded, more than 50% greater than a 1976 Ford Cortina.

One solution to the problems with lithium batteries would be to use a different method for generating electricity such as the fuel cell. This technology was originally developed by NASA for the Gemini spacecraft back in the early sixties. Essentially it consists of a large box containing hydrogen and oxygen separated by a membrane made of platinum and iridium. These two gases react together, to produce water and electricity.

Unfortunately, there are snags with fuel cells. Both platinum and iridium are rare metals which are expensive and in short supply. Also, hydrogen is expensive to manufacture, and requires a lot of energy. That is the same reason that hydrogen-fuelled gas boilers and hydrogen cars may not be practical.

So in summary *electric cars* are not good for the environment. They are not eco-friendly and will not save the planet. And they will eventually become casualties of the government's *War on Cars.*

Chapter 5

The Advantages of Electric Cars

I would now like to consider the claimed advantages of electric cars. They are as follows:

1) No pollution from exhaust fumes

Electric cars don't have an exhaust pipe so obviously they don't contribute to air pollution or CO_2 emissions, but as explained elsewhere in this book, the electricity required to charge them is mostly generated by fossil fuels. Construction of electric cars and their lithium batteries is also associated with a lot of carbon emissions. And the extra weight of electric cars, an additional 500 kg, causes greater tyre wear and air pollution from rubber particles.

2) Better acceleration

Conventional cars have a front-mounted engine which transmits its power through a gearbox, which can be manual, automatic or semi-automatic, and a drive shaft. Electric cars don't require a gearbox and the usual mechanical layout involves four electric motors with each one driving a wheel. This gives the benefits of four-wheel drive which are well-known. Although some of the newer electric cars have only a single electric motor which drives the rear wheels.

The reason electric cars don't need a gearbox is because electric motors produce reasonable power and torque (turning force) even at low revolutions. If you have ever played with a Scalextric set you will remember that you increased the speed of each tiny racing car by increasing the voltage delivered to each car's electric motor via a simple hand control, which was a variable resistor, known as a rheostat. That is how the accelerator in an electric car works.

If you have ever stood on a station platform and watched diesel and electric trains pulling away from the platform, you will notice that electric trains have far better acceleration than diesels. The reason that petrol and diesel cars require a gearbox is because internal combustion engines have to be revved to about 2,500 rpm or more to produce reasonable power. To allow the engine to rev this high at low speeds a gearbox has to be fitted. In the 1930s, three-speed gearboxes were the norm, then — four speed was usual up until the seventies. Now a five-speed gearbox is almost universal for manual gearbox cars, with some cars having six gears.

Electric cars don't have gearboxes, making them easier to drive. However, this design feature has a downside as it makes them difficult to move if they run out of charge. If a petrol or diesel car runs out of fuel then it can still be pushed or towed once the gearbox has been put in neutral. This is not possible in an electric car as it does not have a gearbox. If you try and push an electric car, which has run out of charge, then you will be pushing against the resistance of the motors, that is almost impossible. It is like putting a conventional car into first gear and then trying to push it.

Another advantage of conventional cars with manual gearboxes is that they can extricate themselves from railway level crossings if they break down, by using the starter motor. If you are driving a conventional, petrol or diesel car with a manual gearbox and the engine dies while you are going over a level crossing you can save yourself and the car by putting the car into first gear and then using a series of bursts from the starter motor with the handbrake off. This will work if your car has run out of fuel or the engine has died but obviously not if your battery is flat. Drivers of electric cars cannot do this. So I would advise electric car drivers *not* to go over level crossings if they are running low on charge as there is no way of moving their vehicle quickly if it dies.

For the same reason, electric cars cannot be towed in the conventional way. Breakdown services such as the AA have to use a special device such as a low trailer which fits under an electric car and lifts the wheels off the ground so it can be towed.

.

3) Lower running costs

This would have been a factor in the recent past, but things are changing rapidly. The UK Government used to give electric car drivers a large discount for purchasing a new EV but that scheme has now ended. EV drivers have also been exempt from UK Road Tax, but from 2025, they will be liable for it. Councils used to provide charging points where electric car drivers could charge their vehicles for free, but fees are now being levied in most areas and the fees charged are likely to increase as councils struggle to balance their books.

In any case the price of electricity is likely to go through the roof because of the Ukraine War, inflation and the drive for Net Zero, so any cost savings are likely to vanish and electric cars will probably end up more expensive to run than petrol and diesel vehicles, especially as the costly lithium battery will need to be changed every 5 –10 years at a likely cost of £8,000 or more.

4) Less noise

Electric cars are quiet and this means that city centres will become less noisy. But the quietness of electric cars will itself cause problems. There have been a number of cases where pedestrians have been knocked down by electric cars as they didn't hear them coming. I cycle a lot in the summer months and usually know if a car is behind me because I can hear the engine. But I am usually unaware of an electric car approaching from behind because I cannot hear it. There have already been many well-publicised cases in which a pedestrian in a supermarket car park has been knocked down by a car they didn't hear. And as electric cars are on average 500 kg heavier than a fossil-fuel car they do a lot more damage when they hit a pedestrian or another car.

One solution to this problem would be to fit electric cars with noisemakers so that pedestrians can hear them. This was proposed some years ago but has never been implemented.

Another problem with electric cars is that the engine noise is not pleasant. It is simply an annoying whine. Compare that with the beautiful noise that multi-cylinder petrol engines make. As a general rule, the more cylinders a petrol engine has, the more pleasant the noise. A six-cylinder engine sounds better than a four-cylinder one. And a V8 or V12 engine is even sweeter. Think of the car chase in the Steve McQueen film *Bullitt,* 1968, which involved two V8-engine cars, a Ford Mustang and a Dodge Charger. It is one of the most exciting car chases ever filmed and one of the reasons it works so well is the marvellous sound of the V8 engines being pushed to their limits. If that car chase were re-enacted today with electric cars, it simply wouldn't be thrilling and the two cars would probably run out of charge halfway through the sequence.

Aircraft engines sound even more exciting than car engines. Probably the best-sounding aircraft engine is the Rolls-Royce Merlin V12, which was fitted to the Spitfire, Hurricane, Mosquito and Lancaster and many other aircraft, including later versions of the North American P-51 Mustang. I have seen all these planes fly at air displays. They are always show stoppers. I wonder if in years to come the Net Zero zealots will ban all air displays because of the *climate emergency.*

Conclusion

So that is a summary of all the *advantages* of electric vehicles and as you can see each claimed *advantage* comes with its own snags.

Chapter 6

Battery Problems

In this book I have discussed my reservations about electric cars. But most of the problems with electric cars are caused not by their electric motors but by their use of lithium-ion batteries. Here is a list of the most common problems:

1) Limited range

Modern cars with internal combustion engines have a good range. Jeremy Clarkson once drove a diesel Audi A8 4.0 TDI from London to Edinburgh and back, about 800 miles total, on a single tank of diesel. Even a basic Volkswagen Golf diesel has a quoted range of 888 miles on a full tank. No electric car currently manufactured has a range anything like that. Although a range of over 200 miles has been quoted for some of the more expensive models; in practice a range of 100–150 miles is more likely.

The performance of a lithium battery is affected by ambient temperature because they depend on a chemical reaction. If you understand science you will know that all chemical reactions are slowed down by cold temperatures. That is why cement mortar will not set below five degrees Celsius. This means that lithium batteries offer a shorter range in cold weather.

On 9 March 2023, the *Daily Mail* ran a story, based on a *Which* magazine report, which stated that cold temperatures reduced the effective range of electric cars by a third. The magazine came to this conclusion after testing twelve different EVs from different manufacturers. They were all charged to the maximum and left overnight in cold weather before being started and driven until they stopped. The *Daily Mail* also noted that range would be reduced further if the car's heater was used — who drives with their heater switched off during a British winter?

In freezing temperatures lithium batteries can become impossible to charge. This means that in very cold weather it is difficult for a breakdown service to assist motorists who have broken down because of lack of charge. Their cars cannot be fitted with a fresh, charged battery because it is the size of a king-size mattress. The only solution is to charge the car where it is or tow it away using a special lifting device such as a low trailer which fits under the car and raises the wheels above the road surface. By contrast, fossil fuel car motorists only need a gallon of petrol or diesel from a can and they then have enough fuel to get to the nearest filling station.

2) Lack of public chargers

Between 300,000 and 450,000 public chargers will need to be installed throughout the UK to meet the likely demand for them, but this programme is not proceeding nearly fast enough. In addition many chargers are faulty and are not being repaired at a swift pace. Free chargers are also being phased out by cash-strapped local councils.

3) Charging takes too long

You can fill a car fuel tank with petrol or diesel in a matter of minutes, but charging a lithium battery takes time. You can either use an overnight trickle charger which takes eight to twelve hours or else use a fast charger at a service station which can give you an 80% charge in forty minutes. But even forty minutes is a long time for a car to sit at a service station and this means that long queues of electric vehicles can build up, with drivers waiting for hours to get their cars charged. This was illustrated by a story which made the pages of several British newspapers over the Christmas holidays in 2022 when there were large queues of Tesla cars awaiting charging at a number of filling stations in England.

4) Home charging can be difficult or impossible

It is not difficult to charge your car at home if you have a driveway. But what if you live in a terraced house? The only solution is to trail the bulky charging cables across your pavement resulting in a considerable trip risk to pedestrians, although there is remedy to this as you can have a channel excavated in the pavement. You put your charging cable in this and cover it with a plastic strip.

There are also practical difficulties involved in fitting home charging systems to blocks of flats. And thieves may steal your very expensive charging cable. It is now recommended that you buy a special expensive padlock to protect your charging cable as they are valuable and likely to be stolen.

5) Battery charging levels should ideally be between 10% and 80% to maintain the life of the battery.

Lithium-ion batteries have a lifespan of five to ten years. But after just five years of use their performance diminishes and range decreases. To maintain maximum battery life it is recommended that the battery should never be fully discharged and should remain above 10% charge. In addition, to maintain maximum battery life it should never be fully charged either. 80–90% charge is recommended. But most people setting out on a long journey would probably charge their battery fully because they would be worried about running out of charge because of a lack of charging points.

Battery life will also affect the resale price of an electric car. It has been predicted that most car dealers will be unwilling to accept an electric car more than five years old because they may be faced with the cost of replacing the battery if it fails after they have sold the car to a new owner. It will be difficult and expensive to dispose of used electric car batteries as they cannot be recycled.

6) Fire risk

There have been disturbing reports of lithium-ion batteries catching fire and I have covered this is depth in the chapter entitled, Fire Down Below.

Conclusion

Cars with Lithium-ion batteries are not suitable for long journeys. They are best suited to people who have facilities for home charging and do not use them for long journeys.

Chapter 7

Fire Down Below

As you may have guessed from what I have written so far in this book, I am an aviation buff. Before my life changed completely when I became my wife's carer in 2011 — see one of my other books *A Life By Misadventure*, I used to visit aircraft museums and attend air displays throughout the UK.

One of my favourite aircraft has always been the Boeing B-29 Superfortress. A highlight of Christmas 1965, was one of my presents, the new Airfix 1/72 scale model of the B-29. At the time it was the largest and most detailed model Airfix had ever made. Seventeen years later my first wife bought me the even larger Monogram 1/48 scale B-29 for Christmas. Upon completion it was so big that I could only display the completed model by hanging it from the ceiling of our flat using fishing line.

I have never seen a B-29 Superfortress fly. To do that I would have to travel to the USA where there are two airworthy B29s known as *Fifi* and *Doc*, but I have seen the preserved B-29 at the Imperial War Museum in Duxford, near Cambridge. Known as *It's Hawg Wild,* the aircraft was flown from Arizona to Duxford in early 1980, and then restored to immaculate static condition.

The B-29 is remembered as the aircraft that brought WW2 to an end as it dropped the two atom bombs on Hiroshima and Nagasaki. Conventional bombing raids on Japan by B-29s also greatly weakened Japan in the first few months of 1945.

The B-29 featured a number of technical innovations such as pressurized crew compartments and remote-controlled gun turrets aimed by optical gyro gunsights, which were assisted by analogue computer technology using thermionic valves, aka vacuum tubes. This made the B-29 the best-protected bomber of WW2.

However, even the mighty B-29 had a weakness, namely its engines. It was powered by four Wright R-3350 twin-row, 18-cylinder engines delivering 2,200 horsepower each. But even this was really insufficient power for such a large, heavy aircraft. Another snag was that the engines were tightly cowled to reduce drag. This caused overheating. In addition much of the engine, including the crankshaft, was constructed of a lightweight magnesium alloy which could catch fire. Once a magnesium fire developed it would reach a temperature of 3,100 Celsius, making it impossible to extinguish. The fire would burn through the main spar in minutes, and the aircraft would be lost.

The statistics speak for themselves. 414 B-29s were lost in WW2, but only 147 were brought down by flak and fighters, the other 267 were lost because of engine fires. The B-29's problems were eventually sorted after the war by various engine modifications, but the problems caused by magnesium in engines remains to this day. This is why the two airworthy B-29s in the USA, *Doc* and *Fifi* have had extensive engine modifications to make them safer to operate.

This tendency of the B-29 to suffer engine fires was well known even as prototypes were being tested. On 18 February 1943, Boeing's chief test pilot, Eddie Allen, was killed flying the second prototype B-29 when it developed an engine fire and then crashed into the Frye Meat Packing Plant in Seattle. All the crew aboard the B-29 were killed along with nineteen meat plant workers.

If you understand chemistry you will know that magnesium and lithium are close to each other in the periodic table and thus have similar properties. Like magnesium, lithium can catch fire and burns with a very hot flame which is difficult to extinguish.

So it is no surprise from what I have just said that lithium battery fires are a problem with electric vehicles. In February 2022, the mainstream media covered the story of the 650-foot cargo vessel M.V. *Felicity Ace,* which developed an uncontrollable fire as a result of carrying electric vehicles. The ship was reported as carrying a total of 4,000 cars including 1,100 Porsches and 189 Bentleys. Only some of the vehicles were electric, but that was still enough to cause an uncontrollable fire which led to the loss of the ship.

More recently on 14 February 2023, *The Expose* website carried a lengthy report by Rhoda Wilson, about the Norwegian shipping company, Havila Krystruten, which runs services between Bergen and Kierkenes. The company stated that its vessels were not equipped to tackle lithium-ion battery fires which occurred at sea and banned electric vehicles from its ships.

"This is a pre-safety assessment, and the conclusion of the risk analysis shows that a possible fire in fossil vehicles, i.e. petrol or diesel, can be handled by the systems and crew on board", said Bent Martini, the company's managing director. "A possible fire in electric, hybrid or hydrogen cars will require external rescue efforts and could put people on board and the ships at risk".

'We will never compromise the safety of passengers and crew. When we get such a clear conclusion on the risk assessment, the decision is very simple", said CEO, Arild Myrvoll.

The problem is particularly acute in Norway, which is one of the largest users of electric vehicles. More than 80% of all vehicles sold in Norway in 2022 were fully electric, making this decision a nuisance for passengers.

In 2020, Ford and BMW recalled 46,000 electric vehicles, including 5,000 in the UK. Ford recalled more than 20,000 Kuga plug-in hybrids in August 2022, after it discovered that a number of batteries were overheating when charging, and causing a fire. Owners — including 1,800 in the UK — were advised not to charge their cars and to operate them in *EV Auto* mode only.

BMW has also revealed that it has identified almost 3,000 plug-in hybrid models in the UK that could be at risk of a battery fire. BMW issued a recall and suspended delivery of affected new models as a preventative measure. A total of 26,700 vehicles are said to be involved worldwide of which 2,930 are either with UK customers or awaiting delivery. The German carmaker has said that, "Particles may have entered the battery during the production process, which could lead to a short circuit within the battery cells when it is fully charged. This may lead to a fire."

The Expose website also obtained data for 2019, via a Freedom of Information request which suggested an incident rate for vehicle fires of 0.04% for petrol and diesel cars. The rate for plug-in electric vehicles was 0.1%.

In September 2021, General Motors advised owners of Chevy Bolt EV or Bolt EUVs to park fifty feet away from other vehicles when in a parking garage because of fire risks. The car manufacturer also suggested that owners park their vehicles outdoors and avoid leaving them unattended while charging, owing to the fire risk.

Owners were also advised to limit charging of their vehicle batteries to under 90% capacity using the Target Charge Level mode, to avoid frequent charging sessions and to also avoid depleting the battery below seventy miles range.

Lithium-ion batteries can catch fire or explode when exposed to extreme heat or if punctured or damaged. Firefighters need special training and equipment to tackle electric vehicle fires.

The Fire Brigade is used to dealing with blazes involving cars, trucks and other vehicles but those caused by lithium-ion batteries involve new hazards. During an electric vehicle fire, over a hundred organic chemicals are generated, including toxic gases such as carbon monoxide and hydrogen cyanide, both of which are poisonous. Thus, emergency responders must have appropriate PPE to protect themselves. In addition, electric fires don't respond to traditional fire-extinguishing methods. The burning battery pack is usually inaccessible to externally applied suppressants and can re-ignite without sufficient cooling. The heat from an electric fire is greater than that from a petrol fire, exceeding 2,760 degrees Celsius. Applying water or foam can cause a violent flare up. There is also the risk of an electric shock.

So, in summary, electric cars pose a risk. Petrol and diesel cars can also catch fire, but as you can see from the figures given above EVs have a far greater fire risk.

Chapter 8

Electric Car Horror Stories

For several years the UK Government, and many others around the world, has ensured that only one side of the climate change narrative is presented i.e. that we are doomed unless we do a number of very inconvenient and expensive things such as replacing our gas boilers with heat pumps and driving electric cars. Despite a massive effort to suppress the truth, a large number of stories have appeared in the mainstream media which describe motorists' negative experiences of electric cars. These usually involve the car breaking down in the middle of nowhere with no prospect of immediate rescue, and causing the owner great stress, expense and inconvenience.

The best known of these articles is, *Why I pulled the plug on my electric car* by Giles Coren, which was published in *The Times* on 7 January 2023, and subsequently promulgated on the Internet and reprinted in other publications. Coren was dismayed when his two-year-old £65,000 Jaguar I-Pace, ran out of charge in a rural location over the New Year period and had to be abandoned in a single-track road. The car could not be moved because it could not be put into neutral as it lacked a gearbox — a technical snag of electric cars which I have explained in detail elsewhere in this book.

Coren went on to describe how he first bought the car in late 2020, "in a deluded Thunbergian frenzy", and how it had spent most of the time since at the Jaguar dealer getting various electrical glitches fixed. During these frequent and lengthy periods when the Jag was being repaired, Coren drove diesel courtesy cars supplied by the dealer under the terms of the car's warranty.

He then said that he intended to sell his Jaguar and replace it with a reliable petrol car while there was still time because the electric car industry was, "no more ready to transport people to Cornwall and back at Christmas time ... than it is to fly us all to Jupiter".

Coren criticized the car's range, stating that the claimed 292 miles was 220 miles in practice and that two out of three filling station chargers didn't work. Apps such as Zap Map, which were supposed to direct you to chargers, often didn't work and required 5G, which wasn't available in many parts of the country. He also mentioned that the Society of Motor Manufacturers had pointed out that only twenty-three new chargers were being installed every day in the UK instead of the hundred per day that were planned, despite the number of EV drivers tripling in two years. Another problem was that many roadside chargers were *trickle* chargers rather than *fast* chargers which meant that EVs had to be left plugged in overnight, which required the driver to find a hotel to stay in.

Just three weeks later, on 27 January 2023, the *Daily Mail* carried a two-page article by Tom Rawstorne, that outlined the negative side of electric car ownership. With the title, *How range anxiety, lack of chargers and soaring power costs have sent the Electric Car Revolution into Reverse.* The article featured interviews with a number of drivers who wished they had never bought an electric vehicle.

The article began with the case of Sophie Preston-Hall, who drove from her home in Essex to Blackpool to attend an awards ceremony. This would have taken four-and-a-half hours in a petrol or diesel car but took the businesswoman twelve hours in her new BMW electric car. The vehicle had a claimed range of 180 miles, but in practice this was just 150 miles and even that was achieved only by turning off the heating and demister. This is quite a common practice in EV driving. Because heating, demisting and aircon all work from battery power, these features are often turned off in an electric vehicle to extend its meagre range.

Sophie's problems were caused by a lack of available working chargers. When she arrived at a pre-planned stop at a service station in the Midlands she found that all the chargers were either in use or broken.

"It's an absolute joke," she said. "And it has happened to me again and again. You find a place with a charger and you have to queue ... but when you finally get your turn to use the charger it doesn't work. The infrastructure to support electric cars just isn't here in this country yet."

Tom Rawstorne then revealed that the government was set to miss the target of 300,000 chargers by 2030, by twenty years. Figures from the Department of Transport showed that fewer than 9,000 public charging points have been installed in the past year. There are now thirty electric vehicles for every charge point compared with sixteen at the start of 2020.

Another person who had a bad experience with an electric car was ex-*Blue Peter* presenter, Helen Skelton, who ended up stranded while making her way back to Cumbria and shared her experiences on Instagram.

"Can't charge it and not for the first time … stranded," she wrote.

Rawstorne then revealed that Britishvolt, a new company that was planning to build 300,000 lithium battery packs per year, had gone into administration. In 2015, only one per cent of newly registered vehicles were electric, yet EV's now accounted for one in six of all new registrations with 620,000 EVs on the road.

Rawstorne cited the case of Stephanie Davies, a company secretary who bought a new Audi Q4 e-tron in 2022, and found it did not meet her expectations. For one thing its claimed 210-mile range was not achieved in practice. To get this sort of range she had to turn off as many electrical devices as possible, as many other EV drivers have found. She also found that there were insufficient charging points. On one occasion, with just six miles of battery charge left, she was forced to stop at a Holiday Inn in order to use a fast charger, only to be hit with a £100 parking charge because she wasn't a resident at the hotel. Miss Davies became so fed up with her electric Audi that she planned to ditch it and buy a diesel vehicle. One consideration was that using a fast charger makes your EV almost as expensive to run as a diesel vehicle.

Rawstorne then mentioned the experiences of prison service worker, Karen Karbitz, who bought a Kia Niro EV and experienced similar problems to those described earlier. For example, the claimed 220–240-mile range was not achieved in practice. It was reduced in cold weather and Karbitz found that using the heating, cost twenty-two miles range so she turned it off. Karbitz eventually swapped her EV for a hybrid.

Bakery owner, Kristy Giblin, also described her negative experiences with an electric Vauxhall Mokka. After driving from Northumberland to Harrogate to celebrate her mother's 60th birthday party she intended to charge her car at a charging point near the venue. Unfortunately, another selfish EV owner plugged his vehicle into the only available charging point and left it there for twenty-four hours. This meant that her party experience was ruined as she spent the whole time worrying about how she was going to get the car charged.

The last person interviewed for the *Mail* article was MG4 driver, Mark Vincent, who found himself locked in his vehicle with horn and alarm blaring after the car developed an electrical fault. Despite it still having 35% charge left, he had to be rescued by a mechanic. Mr Vincent has since switched to a petrol vehicle.

Such stories as I have just described are not uncommon and hundreds of them can be found on the Internet. No doubt there are some drivers out there with positive experiences of electrical vehicles but to date I have not found any.

Chapter 9

Global Warming and Climate Change

So why are we being forced to give up fossil-fuelled cars and switch to electric battery-powered vehicles? The reason is alleged *man-made climate change.* According to this dubious theory, the use of fossil fuels since the Industrial Revolution has resulted in vast amounts of carbon dioxide being pumped into the atmosphere.

CO2 comprises only 0.04% of the atmosphere and only 3.2% of it is man-made. It is one of a number of *greenhouse gases* which prevent heat from the atmosphere and Earth's surface from radiating into space. Another *greenhouse gas* is methane, which is one of several reasons why meat-eating is now frowned upon by climate activists. According to this theory, the Earth is gradually warming up, which is causing extreme weather, melting of the icecaps, raising of the sea level, erosion of our coastline, flooding, bushfires, crop failures, heatwaves, famine, deaths and so on. And the only solution, allegedly, is to stop using fossil fuels, phase out gas boilers, stop eating meat and switch to electricity generation using *renewable* sources. Production of petrol and diesel cars must cease and there is a big question mark over the future of the aviation industry, which uses mainly jet and turboprop engines, plus some internal combustion engines in light aircraft. Farming will also be phased out and most of humanity will have to survive on a diet of insects and synthetic laboratory-created food.

It is an immensely complicated subject. I could quite easily write a 1000-page book about climate change and barely scratch the surface of the issue. As this is meant to be a concise tome I have merely covered the main points about the subject but have given a list of books in the *Further Reading* section near the end of the book, which cover the subject in greater detail.

According to some climate scientists there has been a large increase in global temperatures since the end of the 19th century, around the time the internal combustion engine, both petrol and diesel was introduced. A well-known graph which has been widely promulgated, the famous *hockey-stick* graph originally produced by Michael Mann, shows a large uptick in global temperatures starting at the end of the 19th century and continuing relentlessly to this day.

Former British Prime Minister, Boris Johnson, apparently became a convert to the climate change and Net Zero movement after attending a presentation by Chief Scientific Officer, Sir Patrick Vallance, which included the famous hockey-stick graph. Prior to that Johnson had allegedly been a climate change sceptic, once claiming that, "Wind turbines couldn't produce enough electricity to pull the skin off a rice pudding".

However, the famous hockey-stick graph has been criticised by many scientists as the original version did not feature the well-known medieval warming period in the Middle Ages (AD 950 to AD 1250), or times when winters were exceptionally cold and the River Thames froze over. The last time the River Thames froze over was in January 1963, when Britain had its coldest winter in 200 years. But there was a "Little Ice Age" between the early 17th and early 19th centuries when many "Frost Fairs" were held on the Frozen Thames. In order to get round this inconvenient problem some versions of the graph start at the year AD 1200, instead of AD 1000, which is generally accepted as the beginning of the Middle Ages.

The truth is that the Earth's temperature has varied widely for millions of years. We have had ice ages in the past and also periods when the Earth's temperature was very warm and glaciers melted. If the *man-made global warming* theory was correct then we should have seen a constant increase in temperature since the late 19th century with every year being hotter than the previous one. In reality, global warming ran out of steam in the 1990s and the Earth is currently cooling. The hottest year of the 20th century wasn't 1998, as is often claimed, it was 1934. Global warming activists have responded to these revelations by now talking about climate change *rather than* global warming.

So although the world is supposedly getting hotter, far warmer than it has ever been, extreme weather events, including intense cold and snow, are still blamed on climate change, which is the conspiracy theory formerly known as global warming. Does this make sense to you? Me neither.

In short, according to governments and the United Nations, if it rains that is because of climate change. If it doesn't rain that is also because of climate change. If it is hot that is because of climate change. And if it is cold that is because of climate change. *All* extreme weather events are now blamed on man-made climate change and storms are now given names in order to dramatize them. The media has played its part in promulgating the current hysteria. BBC employees are taught to always blame adverse weather events on man-made climate change.

Let us now examine some of the key claims made by the climate change movement:

The ice caps at the North and South Poles are melting because of global warming. Sea levels are rising and we are all going to die if we don't commit to Net Zero immediately.

Not true. The amount of ice at the poles is actually increasing. And sea levels are barely rising.

All the polar bears are dying because of climate change. I have seen film of them drowning. What other proof do you need?

The number of polar bears is at a record high. In 2015, there were 26,000 polar bears. Today there are 30,000. Only four polar bears were involved in a one-off drowning incident in Alaska some years ago which was filmed and received maximum publicity.

But the Great Barrier Reef in Australia is dying. This can only be because of climate change.

No, it is not dying. It has regrown and is in good health.

The level of the River Thames is rising. Soon London will be flooded.

This may appear to be the case, but the reality is that London is subsiding very slightly. This has been going on for a long time but will not cause any problems.

Temperatures are rising inexorably throughout the world. We are all going to die from heatstroke, food shortages and mass migration. As Greta Thunberg has said: "The Planet is on Fire".

A modest increase in average temperatures in cool countries such as the UK would be welcome. More people die of cold than heat every year so a warmer climate would be beneficial, as would an increase in C02, which is an airborne fertiliser. More C02 means more crops and more trees. A greater range of crops could be grown if average temperatures were greater. Hundreds of years ago there were vineyards in England.

There are none at present. And trees absorb a lot of C02 through the process of photosynthesis. In any case the world is actually going through a period of cooling at the moment.

A further complication arises from the way in which we measure temperature. It is very easy to produce a false high temperature reading by not using carefully controlled conditions. Normally a device called a Stevenson Screen is used to obtain temperature readings. This is a louvred box which is designed so that the thermometer is protected from direct sunshine which would otherwise give a false high reading.

Modern cars have outside temperature gauges and I am sure we have all had the experience of seeing a freakishly high reading after leaving our car sitting in direct sunshine for a few hours. But once the car starts moving we get a more accurate reading.

One of the worst places to record temperatures is an airfield or airport because the whole area is constantly being blasted by the hot exhaust from hundreds of jet engines. Yet the Met Office will often use temperature readings obtained at airports, particularly Heathrow, which is one of the busiest in the world, to justify its belief in the rather doubtful global warming theory. Airfields and airports also have acres of flat concrete and tarmac which can heat up because of direct sunlight. You have probably had the experience of walking on a cold but sunny day in winter. Even though the air temperature may be low, if you are wearing a dark jacket you may become too hot because of direct sunlight heating up your clothing.

On 19 July 2022, the British media reported that the hottest ever temperature recorded in Britain, 40.3 Celsius, was logged at RAF Coningsby in Lincolnshire at 4.00 p.m. I actually know RAF Coningsby because I visited it in July 1996, in order to see the aircraft of the RAF Battle of Britain Memorial Flight, namely an Avro Lancaster bomber, several Spitfires and Hurricanes, a Dakota and a Chipmunk. The large airbase is also home to two squadrons of RAF Eurofighter Typhoons, which each have two powerful jet engines spewing out hot exhaust gases.

Most people do not realise just how hot and powerful the exhaust from a jet engine can be. After the Second World War, the Supermarine company, which made the Spitfire, produced an aircraft called the Attacker, an early naval jet fighter intended for operation from both land bases and aircraft carriers. One problem with the Attacker though, was that it had a tail-wheel undercarriage like the Spitfire i.e. when it was sitting on the ground it sat on its tail like a Spitfire rather than having a nose wheel like a modern jet fighter or airliner. This design feature caused problems when the Attacker operated from land bases because the jet blast from the tailpipe melted tarmac runways.

Back in the early nineties a group of American engineers decided to excavate a number of vintage WW2 aircraft, which were buried below thick ice and snow in Greenland. The aircraft, two B17E Flying Fortresses and five P-38E Lightnings, crashed on the ice cap after running out of fuel during a delivery flight to the UK in 1942 — known as Operation Bolero.

By the 1990s, the potential cash value of these unique buried aircraft was substantial, so a mission was launched to recover them. The main problem was how to dig a shaft through the ice from the surface to the deep location of the aircraft. In the end, a jet engine was used as it was the only device which could produce enough heat to melt the ice. A gas space heater simply wouldn't have done the job.

Only a single P-38 was recovered as the two B-17s were badly crushed and it was not cost-effective to recover the other P-38s. However, the one P-38 that was salvaged was eventually restored to airworthy condition and now flies in the USA as *Glacier Girl*.

Ostracised for Telling the Truth

Another myth about climate change is that there is a scientific consensus and that the majority of the world's scientists agree that we have a problem and something needs to be done. That is blatantly untrue because a lot of scientists disagree with the current narrative on climate change. See the *Daily Sceptic* website https://dailysceptic.org or Dr Vernon Coleman's websites www.vernoncoleman.com and www.vernoncoleman.org or *The Expose* website https://expose-news.com where you will find considerable information on this topic. The reason we don't hear from sceptical scientists in the mainstream media is because anyone who speaks out is suppressed, demonised, ostracised and vilified. Indeed anyone who expresses the slightest doubts about the man-made global warming theory is branded a *climate denier,* a term which quite deliberately sounds similar to *holocaust denier.* It should be noted that during the Covid-19 pandemic a lot of people who questioned the excessive, draconian and unscientific public health measures imposed by governments were accused of being *covid deniers.* Some people have even suggested that *climate deniers* should be fined and imprisoned and have their property confiscated.

The mainstream media has played its part in promulgating the current hysteria about climate change as it only ever presents one side of the argument i.e. that dictated by governments, the United Nations, The World Economic Forum and various pressure groups. Almost every statement made by climate activist Greta Thunberg receives maximum publicity while the views of sceptical scientists such as climatologist, Dr Judith Curry, PhD are ignored. The BBC has a similar policy as it refuses to have debates about climate change as it considers the science to be *settled.*

The UK opposition parties are also committed to expensive policies to counter climate change with, Sir Keir Starmer, even suggesting that Net Zero should be achieved by 2035, not 2050. I will be talking more about Net Zero in the next chapter.

CO2 and Global Warming

The key claim of the climate change movement is that the level of CO2 in the atmosphere is increasing because of the burning of fossil fuels. Because of the *greenhouse effect* caused by *greenhouse gases,* mainly carbon dioxide, water and methane, this causes less heat to radiate into space, resulting in the Earth heating up.

But there are a number of flaws to this theory. One is the so-called *saturation effect,* which states that once atmospheric CO2 levels rise above 420 parts per million, there is no further *greenhouse effect.* The easy way to understand this is to consider loft insulation. Once you have a thick layer of insulation in your loft then no further benefit can be obtained by putting even more insulation there because no further heat loss is prevented.

Furthermore some climate scientists such as, Dr Patrick Moore, PhD, believe that atmospheric levels of C02 are actually declining and if measures are taken to reduce C02 emissions then it could lead to the death of all plant life and the end of humanity.

Other scientists have suggested that the rise in C02 levels in the atmosphere is because of heating from the sun. So a rise in global temperatures, which is beneficial, is causing more C02 to be released from the oceans.

And there are other scientists who have criticized current climate models which do not take account of solar activity. It is well known that changes in solar activity, such as sunspots, have a great effect on the Earth's climate through what is known as the *solar wind*.

So it is untrue that there is a *scientific consensus* on man-made global warming and climate change. There are doubts about whether the atmospheric C02 level is actually increasing and about whether this is because of fossil fuels or sea warming. In addition, the role of the Sun in determining our climate is being ignored. That is why I think the current proposals to combat climate change by blocking out the sun's radiation using crystals sprayed into the atmosphere from rockets could be disastrous. I believe it could cause another Ice Age with perpetual winters and the end of humanity.

There is a precedent for this claim. In 1816, Europe and North America never had a summer. Scientists believe this was because of the explosion of the volcano Mount Tambora in April 1815, which lead to a fine aerosol of sulphates in the upper atmosphere, that partially blocked out the sun's radiation.

The Fallacy of Computer Modelling and Forecasting

If there is one lesson I have learnt in life it is that predictions on the future made by so-called *experts* are almost always wrong, particularly if they involve computer modelling.

In the early 19th century scientists predicted that railway trains could not travel faster than 30 mph as humans would be unable to breathe above this speed.

In the mid-19th century scientists predicted that heavier-than-air machines, i.e. aircraft would never fly.

In the late 19th century scientists stated that there was nothing left to invent.

In 1939, *Time* magazine predicted that the Germans could not invade France as the French Army was too strong.

In the early 1970s, Margaret Thatcher stated that there would never be a female prime minister in her lifetime.

In March 2020, Imperial College, London predicted that there would be 550,000 Covid deaths in the UK if the Government did not introduce an immediate lockdown. They also claimed that there would be a huge Covid death toll in Sweden because of its decision not to introduce lockdowns. Both these claims proved untrue.

There are also the doom-laden predictions made by politicians and eco activists over the years on the subject of climate change. Here is a selection:

1972

Bjorn Lornberg of the UN predicted the world had ten years to prevent "an environmental catastrophe".

1982

Mostala K Tolba of the UN predicted an environmental catastrophe by 2000.

1989

The UN predicted a *global disaster* by 1999.

1990

Mostafa K Tolba of the UN, *again* said we must fix climate change by 1995.

2000

The Independent newspaper — 20 March 2000, quotes Dr David Viner of the University of East Anglia who said that in a few years winter snowfall would become "a rare and exciting event". In December 2010, the UK had one of the coldest and snowiest Decembers in living memory.

2004

The Guardian newspaper quoted US President Bush who said that "climate change will destroy us". *The Guardian* also said Britain would have a "Siberian climate" by 2020.

2007

Rajendra Pacauri of the UN said that if there is no action on climate change by 2012, then it would be too late.

2008

Former US vice president, Al Gore, claimed that the Arctic would be ice-free by 2013.

2009

Prince Charles said we have, "96 months to save the world".

2009

On 20 October, *The Independent* newspaper quotes Prince Charles who said we have, "fewer than 50 days to save the planet from catastrophe".

2018

In a Tweet dated 21 June 2018, Greta Thunberg said we have, "only five years to save the planet".

2019

The UN said that there are only 11 years left to prevent irreversible damage due to climate change.

* * *

So you can see a common pattern emerging here. An individual makes an outlandish claim. A few years pass, nothing happens and they make further claims, which also don' come true.

You will also notice a similarity with previous *scares* which never happened. Examples include AIDS — which some scientists and the British Medical Association (BMA) thought would infect the entire population by 2000 — the Millennium Bug, the hole in the ozone layer, salmonella in eggs killing us all et cetera.

Furthermore, up until the early 2000s, climate change scares often centred on the notion that humankind was facing a new Ice Age. Since then we have been brainwashed into accepting the idea that "the world is on fire" and we will soon be facing unbearably high temperatures and a "climate apocalypse".

You may have noticed that Met Office forecasts are notoriously inaccurate even one day ahead. The official line is that weather forecasts are 85% accurate but only up to five days ahead. Beyond that they are often wrong. So how can scientists confidently predict what the weather is going to be like in fifty years when they can't predict it even a few days in advance?

In their book *Scared to Death*, first published in 2007, but revised and updated in 2020, investigative journalists, Christopher Booker and Richard North, include a lengthy chapter on global warming. They note that this alleged threat to humanity meets all the criteria for a *scare* which they define as follows:

1- The source of the danger must be something universal to which almost anyone in the population might be exposed.

2- The nature of the danger it poses must be novel.

3- While the scientific basis for the scare must seem plausible, the threat must contain an element of uncertainty.

4- Society's response to this threat must be disproportionate.

The response to the threat of alleged man-made climate change is, of course, Net Zero and all this entails. In the next chapter I will be examining this in more detail.

Chapter 10

The Madness of Net Zero

One consequence of numerous governments' failure to properly investigate the claims of the climate change movement, and also consider the opinions of more sceptical scientists, is that they are now committed to Net Zero policies, which will be economically ruinous and will destroy the modern lifestyle we all enjoy.

In the UK new petrol and diesel vehicles will be banned from sale by 2030, while hybrid cars will be banned from 2035. The fitting of new gas boilers will be prohibited from 2025, and the UK intends to be Net Zero by 2050, although Labour leader, Keir Starmer, has stated that an incoming Labour Government would bring this forward to 2035. At the time of writing, Labour is riding high in the opinion polls so a Labour Government within two years is almost certain.

Most developed countries have set similar timetables for the implementation of Net Zero. But there are a number of notable exceptions. China and India, on course to become two of the biggest economies in the world, have no intentions of doing anything about carbon emissions in the foreseeable future, though they have indicated that they might consider such a policy by 2050 or 2060. In the meantime both nations are committed to building thousands of coal-fired power stations to meet their energy needs, while continuing to use petrol and diesel vehicles.

And here lies one of the biggest snags of the whole Net Zero plan. Even if the unproven theory of man-made global warming is correct, and many scientists think it is not, then every single country in the world, without exception, would have to take the same measures to reduce carbon emissions in order to have any effect on global temperatures.

China and India contribute 60% of the world's CO_2 emissions, so if they decide *not* to adopt Net Zero policies there would be little effect on overall CO_2 levels in the atmosphere. Britain currently accounts for just 1% of global carbon emissions and the USA about 14%.

Third World countries would also be unable to participate in the Net Zero project as they would not have the funds to implement them. For example, I cannot see electric cars taking off in Africa. Fossil-fuelled cars will be the preferred mode of transport for decades to come and I foresee that many of these will be second-hand vehicles bought from Western countries which have switched to electric cars. Similarly, most Third World countries cannot afford solar panel farms or wind turbines, which are both hideously expensive and inefficient.

It is worrying that so many people in the UK and elsewhere haven't woken up to the true cost of Net Zero. Recently, American Senator Robert F Kennedy junior revealed that the estimated cost of implementing Net Zero in the USA would be fifty trillion dollars. As Britain has roughly a fifth of the population of the USA we can safely assume that the cost to the UK would be ten trillion dollars.

To put that in perspective here are some figures on GDP for 2022:

Entire world   100 trillion dollars

USA   25 trillion dollars

UK   3.4 trillion dollars

The current level of debt in the world is currently 300 trillion dollars. That is itself unsustainable even if we disregard the future cost of Net Zero.

So the USA will have to spend double its current GDP just to meet the cost of Net Zero and the UK will have to do likewise. Obviously these calculations do not take into account likely economic growth over the next three decades, but it is possible that there won't be any between now and 2050 as we are currently in a global recession and the green policies advocated by most governments involve no economic growth plus enormous expenditure. Also, the real cost of any major project involving public expenditure is always greater than the estimated cost. I could give many examples of this such as the Edinburgh Trams' project, railway electrification programmes, various road-building schemes, HS2, the London Underground improvements, warship construction and the Scottish Ferguson Marine ferry fiasco.

So, Net Zero does not just involve making your next car electric and fitting a heat pump. There will be implications for *every* aspect of your life including work, diet, transport, housing, holidays, clothing, healthcare, recreation and so on.

Your gas boiler will have to be replaced by a heat pump. At present the UK Government is trying to play down the cost of fitting one, and suggesting that this might be done for as little as £1500. The true cost of installation, plus everything else that will be required such as new piping, new larger radiators, extra internal and external wall and loft insulation, and new, expensive triple-glazed windows, is likely to be in the region of £100,000 per home. How many people have £100,000 in the bank? In practice a second mortgage will be required to pay for this expensive and unnecessary nonsense.

Heat pumps are sometimes referred to as *reverse-phase air conditioners* as they use the same gas law principles as aircon, but to produce heat rather than cold. You have probably seen air conditioning units when you have been on a foreign holiday. There is a large metal box outside the property containing a fan which blows hot air into the atmosphere. This is connected by pipes to other units inside the building which blow cold, refrigerated air. Usually, there is one of these in each room.

Air conditioning units work like domestic refrigerators. Both contain a special refrigerant gas which is compressed by an electric pump to turn it into liquid. This causes a release of heat, which is expelled to the outside air in the case of aircon, or radiates from the back of a fridge. That is the reason that fridges actually warm the room they are in. The very cold liquid that has been created then passes through a heat exchanger in order to cool the fridge interior and the freezer. You can demonstrate this phenomenon by working a bicycle pump. You will notice that the repeated compression of the air in the pump causes a release of heat. So a fridge has a cool interior but actually radiates heat from the back. An air conditioning unit is effectively a fridge interior with a fan to blow the refrigerated air into the room.

A heat pump uses the same basic principle but in reverse. It produces hot air inside the house and cold air outside. This hot air warms water which is pumped around the house the same as in a normal central heating system.

There are two types of heat pump, namely an air source heat pump and a ground source pump. An air source heat pump captures any heat in the atmosphere, even on a cold winter's day, and then uses it to produce warmth by compressing the air. To understand this you have to realize that there is really no such thing as *hot* and *cold* in physics, only degrees of heat. Heat is caused by molecular movement and at any temperature above absolute zero, (minus 273 Celsius), there is some degree of molecular movement.

There is another type of heat pump called a ground source heat pump which captures underground (geothermal) heat using loops of piping. Depending on the design of the installation this can be anything from one metre to one hundred metres below the surface, so a lot of excavation is required. You have probably noticed that it is quite warm in the London Underground even in winter, and sometimes unbearably hot in the summer. That is caused by geothermal heat which is captured by a ground source heat pump.

However, there are a number of snags to heat pumps which are as follows:

1) They are expensive to buy and fit. As well as the heat pump unit they may need new piping throughout the house, new larger radiators, because the water is not as hot as with conventional central heating, and improved insulation including loft insulation, internal and external wall insulation and new triple glazing. In some properties expensive underfloor heating may have to be fitted, which will require all carpets, underlay and floorboards to be lifted.

2) They take a long time to warm a house.

3) They don't make houses very warm. You will have to accept a room temperature of 16 rather than 20 or 21 Celsius, that will require you to wear more clothing indoors in the winter months.

4) Similarly, with a heat pump the hot water won't be warm enough for a comfortable shower or bath.

5) They require a lot of outdoor space, particularly with a ground source heat pump. They make better sense if fitted to a new-build home but are likely to be impossible to fit to many older properties. Flats will also be a problem as each individual property will need a large heat pump cabinet sitting on the ground and there may be insufficient space for this.

6) They are noisy. A number of people who have had them fitted have described the noise as being like a jet engine starting up. So *noise pollution* will be a problem with heat pumps.

7) Lack of electricity generating capacity. This will be a big problem with the Net Zero proposals. If all vehicles are going to be electric and most heating is obtained via heat pumps them there will need to be a huge increase in the UK's electricity generating capacity, possibly a tripling of output. This will require all power transmission cables to be renewed to a thicker type which can handle more current. Every urban street in Britain will have to be dug up to install thicker cabling. And all high-tension cables and pylons will have to be replaced.

The only advantages of heat pumps are that they do not directly emit carbon emissions and they can be cheaper to run than gas boilers.

Of course heat pumps are not the only alternative. Another option would be hydrogen boilers which don't produce any emissions other than water, which can be vented into the atmosphere without causing any problems. Unfortunately there aren't vast reserves of underground hydrogen sitting around waiting to be tapped. Natural gas contains mainly methane, which releases carbon dioxide and carbon monoxide when burnt. The original gas used in gas appliances from the 19th century was coal gas made by heating coal. This contains a lot of hydrogen but also many other substances including carbon dioxide and carbon monoxide.

Pure hydrogen can be manufactured from coal, oil or natural gas, but this requires a lot of energy. It can also be obtained by the electrolysis of water, but this also needs considerable electric power which will be in short supply in the future.

Problems with Electricity Generation

It is really the options for the future generation of electricity that are the major snags of Net Zero. The original method of generating electricity used in the UK and elsewhere since the late 19th century involved burning coal, which fuelled triple expansion piston steam engines which rotated large dynamos. Later, more powerful and efficient steam turbines were used. Peat has also been used in other countries such as Ireland, which has a good supply.

However, climate activists now regard coal as the very worst way of generating electricity as it produces a lot of CO2. For some years Britain has been closing down all of its coal-fired power stations and even demolishing them. Recently, it was announced that the UK will be keeping its last five remaining coal-fired power stations in operation for a further year because of the current energy crisis caused by the Ukraine War. It would have been sensible to simply *mothball* all the coal-fired power stations until new reliable methods of power generation had been set up, but that possibility did not occur to the UK Government.

So, British coal-fired power stations are now almost extinct with gas and oil-fired plants continuing for the time being. There has been much talk about our future energy needs being supplied by *renewables* such as wind, solar, hydro and wave power, but these have their snags, particularly wind power.

Thousands of wind turbines have now been erected throughout the UK and Green politicians get very excited about them. One claim that is often made is that they are highly cost-effective as *wind is free*. In reality nothing could be further from the truth.

Wind turbines are expensive to build and erect and use huge quantities of steel, the manufacture of which uses vast amounts of coking coal, water and electricity. They are therefore associated with a huge amount of carbon emissions.

They don't produce electricity when there is no wind and when the wind is too strong they have to be switched off to prevent damage. They also have to be backed up by fossil-fuelled power stations, which have to be kept on standby mode, burning fuel so that there is no interruption in supply.

Wind turbines also produce a very small amount of electricity, supposedly 2MW each, but in practice much less than this. This compares with 4,000MW for a medium/large sized fossil-fuel power station. So up to 2,000 wind turbines will be needed to produce the same electricity as one conventional power station. Wind turbines are also ugly and a blight on the landscape. They produce a loud noise which can make people ill and they also kill a lot of birds. In conclusion they are definitely *not* the answer to the country's energy problems.

Another controversial method of energy production is 'bio-mass' and the best example of this is the Drax Power Station in Yorkshire. This was originally built as a coal-fired power station but switched to bio-mass some years ago.

Bio-mass involves burning wood pellets, which are prepared by chopping down large trees in the USA and Canada and then transporting them by diesel truck or diesel train to ports on the east coast of North America. Prior to leaving North America the trees are turned into fuel pellets. These are then shipped across the Atlantic in enormous cargo vessels which consume vast amounts of diesel fuel and are then transported to the Drax Power Station by diesel train. The pellets are then burnt in order to generate electricity. They are classed as *renewable* energy because new trees can be planted and grow in their place.

The only problem is that this process can take a very long time. Some trees can take decades to mature and there are even some which have lived for 5,000 years so there is no immediate *renewal.* Even climate activist, Greta Thurnberg, has criticised bio-mass saying that "trees are not renewable". They actually absorb CO_2 from the air through the process of photosynthesis so bio-mass, which involves destroying trees to create fuel, must be one of the dumbest ideas ever conceived.

Some power stations now use bio-fuel which is manufactured from crops such as wheat and corn. Although this results in less CO_2 emissions, it is surely not a good idea to turn precious crops into fuel at a time when the world is facing food shortages for reasons which I will explain shortly.

There is also a tentative plan to build a huge solar farm in Morocco, where the sun shines most days, and then transfer the electricity generated to Britain via an undersea cable. This could possibly be augmented by a large wind farm in the Atlas Mountains. The snags of this scheme are that it would be mega-expensive and the undersea cable would be vulnerable to attack from terrorists or an unfriendly foreign power.

Solar panels produce electricity during daylight hours but none at night. Unfortunately at present there is no way of storing surplus electricity produced during the day. In theory this could be stored in huge *battery farms* extending over many square miles, but this technology would be hugely expensive and probably impractical in view of the likely future shortage of lithium.

One possible solution to the energy crisis would involve building lots of nuclear power stations, but the UK government has only committed to one new nuclear plant so far, and the Scottish Government doesn't want any as it opposes nuclear power. Scotland does have a number of hydro-electric power stations built in the 1950s, but there is little scope for more as they can only be built near high mountains and most of the suitable sites have already been used.

But Net Zero doesn't only involve electric cars and power generation. It will affect every aspect of our lives. The forthcoming ban on new oil exploration will have devastating consequences for everyone because oil isn't just fuel, it is used to create thousands of different products such as clothes, pharmaceutical products, lubricants and plastics.

Mobile phones, computers, iPads and laptops are all made with plastic. They also use metals such as steel, copper, silver and gold which have to be mined. It is difficult to see how manufacture of just about anything could continue if there was a ban on carbon emissions.

A lot of water, iron, coal and electricity is required to make steel which is needed to make just about everything. In the future there will have to be greater recycling of steel and other metals as the world is running short of natural resources. Building cement (mortar) will be a problem as there is no way of making it that is not associated with huge carbon emissions.

Food production will be affected. Climate change activists, backed by the United Nations, the World Economic Forum and most governments are doing their best to put as many farms out of business as possible for a variety of reasons.

This is because farming is associated with huge amount of C02 emissions. Even a single cow consumes a vast amount of water and grass during its lifetime. And they fart a lot, which results in a lot of methane, a greenhouse gas, being discharged into the atmosphere, allegedly worsening global warming. Production of lamb and beef in particular is associated with huge carbon emissions.

The British Government currently offers farmers financial incentives in the region of £100,000 to £150,000 to close their farms and *rewild* their land to supposedly lessen climate change. In Holland over 1,000 farms have been closed down by the government and there have been protests by farmers.

The ultimate aim of governments round the world, backed by the United Nations, is to close all farms and have the entire population, except for a chosen elite, which includes politicians, dining on insects and laboratory-created synthetic food.

Governments around the world are now working on a digital ID system in which every person will have all their personal information stored on their phone. This will include details of their medical record, including vaccinations, and their personal carbon footprint. People will be coerced into living in *15-minute cities* in which everything you need will be within a fifteen-minute walk. People will travel locally by foot or on a bike, and car ownership will eventually be banned.

It is likely that domestic pets will be banned as well, and possibly culled as they cause C02 emissions and there may even be attempts to reduce the size of the population as some leading climate activists have suggested that global warming can only be combated by a drastic reduction in the size of the population. I will leave you to imagine how this might be achieved.

So, in conclusion Net Zero will involve the entire developed world committing economic suicide in order to prevent something which is probably not going to happen. There isn't enough money in the entire world to pay for Net Zero and there will be no economic benefits to *going green.* People need to wake up to what is going on before it is too late.

Chapter 11

How Will *Net Zero* Affect Other Modes of Transport?

This book largely investigates battery-powered electric cars. But how will the Net Zero proposals affect other modes of transport?

Trains

Electric trains, which receive their current from overhead wires, or sometimes from one or two *power rails* on the track, have been around for decades and don't have all the disadvantages of electric cars. So you would think that an obvious answer to the Net Zero plans would be to convert every mile of railway track to electric operation.

But we are much further from that goal than most people realise. Only 38% of railway track in the UK is electrified. In Scotland, which has two Green ministers in its SNP Government, that figure is actually less at 25.3%. The problem is that electrification of railway track is costly and time-consuming, often taking years longer than planned, and usually going over budget.

So diesel trains will be with us for many years to come. In Scotland the SNP-run Scotrail is currently operating refurbished HST (model 125) diesel trains on long-distance routes within Scotland such as Glasgow and Edinburgh to Aberdeen and Inverness. The trains are old, a number first entered service in 1976, and are the same type used on the east-coast line until recently. The original plan was to use them for about a decade until the routes involved were electrified, but the likelihood is that this will take longer than planned and go over budget so the 125s may be in service well into the 2030s.

Meanwhile in England the government has had to delay completion of the mega-expensive HS2 high-speed railway to save money. On 10 March 2023, the *Daily Mail* featured an article entitled *HS2 link shunted into sidings for two years,* in which Political Correspondent, David Churchill, described how the Birmingham to Crewe section of that controversial and expensive project was being delayed for two years to save money. Churchill also suggested that the Manchester to Crewe section of HS2 might also be delayed with a possible opening date of 2043.

Shipping

Most commercial shipping uses huge diesel engines. Navies also use a lot of diesel craft with gas turbines being employed for faster vessels such as frigates, destroyers and cruisers. Some submarines, including the Royal Navy's entire submarine fleet, have nuclear power plants while all the US Navy's submarines and its larger aircraft carriers (aka supercarriers) have nuclear power plants.

Nuclear power has been used in a number of civilian vessels. In 1953, President Dwight D Eisenhower, made his famous "Atoms for Peace" speech. Eisenhower wanted to show that atomic energy could be used for peaceful purposes and not just to make bombs.

One consequence of this policy was the building of a civilian, nuclear-powered vessel called the NV *Savannah*. This was constructed in the late 1950s, and certainly looked impressive. It was 600 feet long and weighed 12,000 tons with sleek, futuristic lines. Ostensibly a cargo vessel, it also doubled as a passenger liner with many luxurious cabins and a swimming pool. In 1964, it made a goodwill visit to Europe.

One problem with the *Savannah* though, was that it produced nuclear waste, some of which had to be dumped in the sea as the vessel didn't have enough storage space for such material. Three other civilian nuclear ships were built, namely the German *Otto Hahn*, the Japanese *Mutsu* and the Russian ice-breaker *Sevmorput,* but the general opinion at the time was that they were an interesting experiment but not really practical in the long-term. One problem with nuclear ships is that they contain a lot of radioactive material, which can cause an environmental disaster if they sink, or are involved in a collision. They also have a habit of leaking radioactive material into the sea. However, with the current energy crisis and the drive for Net Zero it is possible that nuclear ships may make a comeback.

Sailing Ships

It is also possible that, in the future, cargo vessels may be fitted with large sails, not necessarily as a primary method of propulsion but to augment the main engine. The main problem with pure sail vessels is that they can become becalmed if there is no wind. The solution is to have a second method of propulsion using some kind of engine. This is already common practice in the world of tall ships and yachts where a number of vessels have a diesel engine and propeller as a back-up.

Many 19th century ships had both wind and steam propulsion. Isambard Kingdom Brunel's three great ships *SS Great Western*, *SS Great Britain* and *SS Great Eastern* were thus equipped and at one point in her career SS *Great Eastern* was operated on wind power only. So I think this idea may make a comeback as a way of saving fuel.

Electric battery-powered ships are a theoretical possibility, but I can foresee a lot of problems with them as they would require massive banks of huge batteries containing enormous amounts of lithium, which will be in short supply. And there would be the problems with charging which I have described elsewhere.

Aircraft

I have already described the various types of engine which currently power aircraft. But what will happen in the future? Aircraft jet engines emit a lot of C02, so they are already a target for Green activists, some of whom want the entire aviation industry closed down.

Electric aircraft already exist but have the same snags as electric cars. A few years ago a de Havilland Canada Beaver aircraft flew with a 750-horsepower electric motor, but its range was only 160 kilometres. And that is the biggest problem with electric planes — range. Because any aircraft, even one powered by fossil fuel, has to carry extra fuel so that it can divert to another airfield which might be 30–60 minutes flying time away. Usually they have to carry enough extra fuel to remain aloft for at least another hour or two.

This isn't such a problem for a light aircraft, which can in an emergency, land in a field, a golf course, a racecourse, a beach or even a road. Many emergency landings have been carried out in such situations, usually without any problems. But large airliners can only put down on another airfield with a long runway which may be 30–60 minutes flying time away. So an electric airliner with a range of 180 km might have a maximum practical range of 100 km or less for safety reasons.

Another problem is the weight of batteries that an electric aircraft would have to carry. With a conventionally-fuelled airliner, the plane takes off with a full fuel load and lands with its tanks almost empty. Landing with full fuel tanks is dangerous, so aircraft that are about to make an emergency landing are usually required to circle to burn up fuel and only land when their tanks are almost empty. Some wartime RAF bombers such as the Vickers Wellington and the Handley Page Halifax were fitted with underwing, fuel jettison pipes so that they could dump surplus petrol before an emergency landing. But electric airliners could not dump their batteries to make landings safer, so they would always be making heavy landings, which would increase the risk of accidents.

Nuclear Aircraft

During the 1950s, the US Air Force experimented with nuclear jet aircraft propulsion, using a converted Convair B-36 Peacemaker bomber. This used modified jet engines, but instead of kerosene, an inbuilt nuclear reactor provided the heat to work the gas turbines. These engines worked but had a tendency to discharge nuclear waste out of their tailpipes. In addition, a crash would result in an environmental catastrophe so the experiments were abandoned in the late 1950s, after air-to-air refuelling was developed for B-52 bombers, which greatly extended their range.

Zero Emission Jet Engines

A more promising development is the zero-emission jet engine. There are two alternatives namely bio-fuel made from crops, which is really low-emission, rather than zero emission, and hydrogen-fuelled jet engines.

Again there are snags. Recently it was estimated that powering all jet engines with bio-fuel would require half of all crops to be used to create the fuel. Rolls-Royce recently demonstrated a zero-emission gas turbine which runs on hydrogen. The only problem here is that the creation of sufficient hydrogen uses a lot of energy and electricity, both of which will be in short supply in the future. That will also be the main problem with hydrogen central heating boilers and hydrogen fuelled cars.

Conclusion

In summary, the shipping and aviation industries both face a lot of problems as there are no practical alternatives to fossil fuel at present.

Further Reading

Books — all available from Amazon

Zina Cohen — *Greta's homework: 101 Truths about Climate Change that everyone should read* — 2010

David Craig — *There is No Climate Crisis* — 2021

Ed Begley PhD — *Climate Miracle: There is no Climate Crisis* — 2020

Francis Battaglia — *There is no Climate Emergency* — 2021

Vernon Coleman — *Endgame: The Hidden Agenda 21* — 2021

Ross Clark — *Net Zero: How an Irrational Target will Impoverish You, Help China (and Won't Even Save the Planet)* — 2021.

Reports:

UK FIRES Report on achieving Absolute Zero

https://ukfires.org/absolute-zero

Click to Download the report.

This report is worth reading. It includes the proposal that Britain will have just three airports, Heathrow, Glasgow and Belfast open by 2029, with even these three closing by 2050.

Websites:

https://expose – news.com

https ://daily sceptic.org

www.vernoncoleman.com

www.vernoncoleman.org

About the Author

Colin Barron was born in Greenock, Scotland in 1956. He was educated at Greenock Academy (1961–74) and Glasgow University (1974–79) where he graduated in Medicine (M.B. Ch.B.) in July 1979. He worked for the next five years in hospital medicine, eventually becoming a registrar in ophthalmology at Gartnavel General Hospital and Glasgow Eye Infirmary.

In December 1984, he left the National Health Service to set up Ashlea Nursing Home in Callander, which he established with his first wife and ran until 1999. He was the chairman of the Scottish branch of the British Federation of Care Home Proprietors (BFCHP) from 1985 to 1991, and then a founding member and chairman of the Scottish Association of Care Home Owners (SACHO) from 1991 to 1999.

Colin has always had a special interest in writing — his first non-fiction book *Running Your Own Private Residential and Nursing Home* was published by Jessica Kingsley Publishers in 1990. When he was at Glasgow University he was editor of *SURGO* (Glasgow University Medical Journal) between 1977 and 1979. *SURGO* subsequently won an award from *The Glasgow Herald* for best student magazine in 1979. In late 1978 Colin was asked to write an article *How to Improve a Student Medical Journal* which appeared in the *British Medical Journal* in March 1979, and has been reprinted and revised in three separate editions of the BMA's *How To Do It* book.

He was also the art editor and motoring correspondent of *Glasgow Medicine* between 1984 and 1986. He is a former cartoonist, having contributed to *Glasgow University Guardian, Ygorra, Glasgow Medicine, Scottish Medicine* and *BMA News Review*. In February 1977, the Greenock Arts Guild held an exhibition of his work along with that of two other local cartoonists.

He has also written about 150 articles for various publications including *This Caring Business, The Glasgow Herald, Caring Times, Care Weekly, The British Medical Journal, The Hypnotherapist, The Thought Field* and many others. He was a regular columnist for *This Caring Business* between 1991 and 1999, and the editor of *SACHO Newsline* between 1991 and 1999.

Hypnosis and alternative medicine have also been areas of special significance for Colin. In 1999, he completed a one-year diploma course in hypnotherapy and neuro-linguistic programming with the British Society of Clinical and Medical Ericksonian Hypnosis (BSCMEH), an organisation created by Stephen Brooks, who was the first person in the UK to teach Ericksonian Hypnosis. He has also trained with the British Society of Medical and Dental Hypnosis (BSMDH), and with Valerie Austin, a top Harley Street hypnotherapist. Colin has also been a licensed NLP practitioner. In 1992, he was made a fellow of the Royal Society of Health (FRSH). He is a former member of various societies including the British Society of Medical and Dental Hypnosis, Scotland (BSMDH), the

British Thought Field Therapy Association (BTFTA), the Association for Thought Field Therapy (ATFT), the British Complementary Medicine Association (BCMA) and the Hypnotherapy Association.

Colin trained in Thought Field Therapy (TFT) in early 2000, and in November 2001, he became the first British person to qualify as a Voice Technology TFT practitioner. He worked from home in Dunblane and at the Glasgow Nuffield Hospital.

Colin has also had 40 years of experience in public speaking and trained with the John May School of Public Speaking in London, in January 1990.

In May 2011, his wife Vivien, then 55, collapsed at home because of a massive stroke caused by a previously undiagnosed heart tumour known as an atrial myxoma. Colin then became his wife's carer but continued to see a few hypnotherapy and TFT clients. In late July 2015, Colin suffered a severe heart attack and was rushed to hospital. Investigation showed that he had suffered a rare and very serious complication of myocardial infarction known as a ventricular septal defect (VSD), effectively a large hole between the two main pumping chambers of the heart.

Colin underwent open heart surgery to repair the defect in August 2015, but this first operation was unsuccessful and a second procedure had to be carried out three months later. On November 30, he was finally discharged after spending four months in hospital.

As a result of his wife's care needs, and his own health problems, Colin closed his hypnotherapy and TFT business in April 2016, to concentrate on writing books and looking after his wife. His second book *The Craft of Public Speaking* was published on 30 June 2016, and was followed by *Planes on Film* (2016), *Die Harder: Action Movies of the*

80s (2017), *A Life By Misadventure* (2017), *Battles on Screen: WW2 Action Movies* (2017), *Practical Hypnotherapy* (2018), *Operation Archer* (2018), *Victories at Sea: On Films and TV* (2018), and *Travels in Time: The History of Time Travel Cinema* (2019), Codename Enigma (2019), *24 Hours to Doomsday* (2021), and *Four Minutes to Zero* (2022).

His interests include walking, cycling, military history, aviation, plastic modelling and reading. He can be contacted via his website www.colinbarron.co.uk

Printed in Great Britain
by Amazon